Digital Reference Service in the New Millennium

Planning, Management, and Evaluation

Edited by

R. David Lankes
John W. Collins III
Abby S. Kasowitz

The New Library Series
Number 6

Neal-Schuman Publishers, Inc.
New York   **London**

The New Library Series

No. 1 – *Finding Common Ground: Creating the Library of the Future without Diminishing the Library of the Past.* Edited by Cheryl LaGuardia and Barbara A. Mitchell.

No. 2 – *Recreating the Academic Library: Breaking Virtual Ground.* Edited by Cheryl LaGuardia.

No. 3 – *Becoming a Library Teacher.* By Cheryl LaGuardia and Christine K. Oka.

No. 4 – *Teaching the New Library to Today's Users: Reaching International, Minority, Senior Citizens, Gay/Lesbian, First-Generation College, At-Risk, Graduate and Returning Students, and Distance Learners.* Edited by Trudi E. Jacobson and Helene C. Williams.

No. 5 – *Designing, Building, and Teaching in the Electronic Library Classroom.* By Cheryl LaGuardia and John Vasi.

No. 6 – *Digital Reference Service in the New Millennium: Planning, Management, and Evaluation.* Edited by R. David Lankes, John W. Collins III, and Abby S. Kasowitz.

Published by Neal-Schuman Publishers, Inc.
100 Varick Street
New York, NY 10013

∞™ The paper used in this publication meets the minimum requirements of American National Standard for Information Sciences—Permanence of Paper for Printed Library Materials, ANSI Z39.48—1984.
Manufactured in the United States of America.

Library of Congress Cataloging-in-Publication Data

Digital reference service in the new millenium : planning, management, and evaluation / edited by R. David Lankes, John W. Collins III, Abby S. Kasowitz ; foreword by Charles R. McClure.
    p. cm. — (The new library series ; no. 6)
    ISBN 1-55570-384-4 (alk. paper)
    1. Electronic reference services (Libraries)—United States—Planning. 2. Electronic reference services (Libraries)—United States—Management. 3. Electronic reference services (Libraries)—United States—Evaluation. I. Lankes, R. David. II. Collins, John W., 1948- III. Kasowitz, Abby S. IV. Series.

Z711.45 .D54 2000
025.5'24—Dc21   00-056235

DEDICATION

This book is dedicated to Riley.

Contents

List of Tables

List of Figures

Foreword

Only a few years ago, the term "digital reference" would have been unknown. Today, digital reference is likely to become a mainstay of electronic and networked services. What it is, how it operates, why it is important, and how we can improve it are all addressed in this outstanding new publication by R. David Lankes, John W. Collins III, and Abby S. Kasowitz.

Digital reference can no longer be considered the future of librarianship. Digital reference is *now*. Every day, people rely on the Internet for answers to reference questions. Librarians and information professionals have an important opportunity to provide remote reference service to their patrons and the general public and to set standards for quality information service.

Digital reference introduces new issues and reopens old issues in the practice of reference service, including audiences served, technology used, skills required, and policies necessary. Digital reference forces us to question our long-held assumptions about the reference desk, the reference interview, and the role of the professional reference librarian. Indeed, the whole notion of 24/7 (24 hours a day, 7 days a week) digital reference services opens new doors for innovative services. It is clear that the massive shifts in practice brought on by the Internet have not spared the reference staff. Change is here and every library professional must be ready.

Lankes, Collins, and Kasowitz have succeeded in capturing the essence of this evolving field first through the Virtual Reference Desk Digital Reference Conference and now through this book. The Virtual Reference Desk Project <*www.vrd.org*> has been a pioneer in digital reference and one of the foremost efforts to better understand and use digital reference for the networked environment. The editors have a broad range of experience in this field and bring their considerable knowledge of digital reference and librarianship to the work. They have brought together a wide variety of experts from a number of different fields—experts that also have considerable knowledge and expertise on the topic.

Digital Reference Service in the New Millennium: Planning, Management, and Evaluation blends both academic discussion and pragmatic experiences in the area of digital reference. Those looking for a better understanding of the facets of digital reference and those looking for "how to do it" will both be satisfied with this book. Moreover, the book will tantalize readers with the opportunities and possibilities for the next generation of digital reference services. Just think, digital reference that is interactive video, or real-time virtual reality experiential learning! These are but a few of the possibilities that lie ahead.

This book represents the first systematic exploration of digital reference. It provides not only a snapshot of the emerging field of digital reference, but an outline of the work yet to be done. It also captures the thoughts of the new thinkers in reference. It represents an exciting and new set of issues that will cause us all to rethink "reference services" as the networked environment continues to evolve. As the field of digital reference continues to grow and change, this book will be looked upon as one of the seminal works in the field.

CHARLES R. MCCLURE,
Francis Eppes Professor and Director
Information Use Management and Policy Institute
School of Information Studies
Florida State University

Preface

The chapters that follow grew out of the "Reference in the New Millennium" conference held at Harvard University. The chapters selected for inclusion represent cutting edge thinking by leading experts in the field. The editors of this volume recognized early on the significance of the information they were gathering and committed to publishing this book as quickly as possible. The book addresses a critical need for information on this topic. This was evident from the outset as the conference call for papers generated a huge response and became extremely competitive. As a result, a highly selective process for inclusion was developed and permission to publish the selected papers was obtained as papers were chosen for presentation at the conference.

Intended for librarians and other information professionals, *Digital Reference Service in the New Millennium: Planning, Management, and Evaluation* focuses both on the theoretical aspects of defining digital reference services in the new millennium, and the evolving service and technical aspects of developing, managing, and evaluating them.

Digital reference is examined in a variety of settings, including the public and private sectors, profit and not-for-profit services, as well as government, academic, public and school libraries, and information services. Collectively, the experts gathered at the first Virtual Reference Desk Digital Reference Conference to explore all aspects of this exciting and evolving phenomenon and share their experiences.

This book is arranged thematically. The first section, "The Foundations of Digital Reference", looks at the traits and trends of a newly emerging reference culture. Chapters within this section focus on transformations and definitions of reference in new contexts and offer a theoretical framework for the sections that follow.

The middle sections, "Building Digital Reference Services and Networks", "Managing Digital References Services", and "Evaluating Digital Reference Services", offer practical advice; including discussions of standards, quality assessments, scalability, technology, and intellectual property issues. The section on evaluation discusses methods for assessing digital reference services and results of research studies conducted on two services.

The last section provides an examination of three existing digital reference services in a variety of libraries and locations: public libraries in Southern California, The University of North Texas Library, and The University of Calgary (Canada) Library. Their use highlights specific technologies to deliver service.

A bibliography of articles and other resources about digital reference technologies and practices completes the volume and will be kept up to date at *<www.vrd.org/pubinfo/proceedings99_bib.html>*.

The purpose of this book is to provide access to the best current critical thinking about digital reference services. The "Reference in the New Millenium" conference was organized by the Virtual Reference Desk (VRD), a project of the United States Department of Education. The conference planners, recognizing the need to bring people and organizations together to focus collective expertise on issues relating to emerging digital reference services, assembled an impressive list of individual presenters and organizational sponsors. The conference was part of the National Education Network's Forum Series and sponsorship for the conference included support from the White House Office of Science and Technology Policy, the National Library of Education, the Library of Congress, the ERIC Clearinghouse on Information and Technology, NELINET, and the Monroe C. Gutman Library at Harvard University. Presenters represented organizations from a diverse group of organizations including academic institutions such as the University of California, the Georgia Institute of Technology, the University of Calgary, and many others. Other organizations included the Library of Congress, the Census Bureau, and the Los Angeles Public Library. Digital reference services including the MAD Scientists Network, AskERIC, and the Virtual Reference Desk rounded out the line-up.

Readers of *Digital Reference Service in the New Millennium: Planning, Management, and Evaluation* will come away with a deep understanding of the issues, both theoretical and practical, relating to digital reference services. The book can also be used as a "how to" guide and reference book. The many existing programs presented can be viewed as models for new and developing services. Readers new to the field as well as those already managing reference services of this nature will find valuable information and advice from leading thinkers and practitioners in the emerging field of digital reference.

JOHN W. COLLINS III

Acknowledgments

The editors would like to thank everyone who contributed to the success of the Virtual Reference Desk 1999 Digital Reference Conference. They include:

Conference sponsors: the White House Office of Science and Technology Policy, the Department of Education's National Library of Education, the Library of Congress, and the ERIC Clearinghouse on Information and Technology.

The National Education Network for their support of the Digital Reference Awards Ceremony, audiotaping and transcription of all sessions, conference program printing, and other items.

The Monroe C. Gutman Library at the Harvard Graduate School of Education and the staff of the Harvard Graduate School of Education Gutman Conference Center for their assistance before and during the conference.

NELINET for their assistance with publicity and registration.

The Conference 1999 Planning and Implementation Committee at the Information Institute of Syracuse—Blythe Bennett, Joann Wasik, Joanne Silverstein, Sue Wurster, Marilyn Schick, and Pauline Lynch.

All conference speakers, presenters, and panel participants.

We would also like to thank those who assisted with preparing this manuscript: freelance editor Nicole Catgenova, abstractor

Marilyn Smith, indexer Laurie Winship, and Neal-Schuman Publishers series editor Cheryl LaGuardia.

R. DAVID LANKES,
JOHN W. COLLINS III, and
ABBY S. KASOWITZ
Syracuse, New York, May 2000

Introduction

The Foundations of Digital Reference

R. David Lankes

This chapter outlines the emerging field of digital reference. It examines the changing roles of reference staff. It also examines two key issues that digital reference services must face: scalability *(the ability for services to grow) and* ambiguity *(identifying the resources needed to meet users' needs before answering a question). A series of digital reference approaches are examined in terms of these issues.*

THE EMERGING FIELD OF DIGITAL REFERENCE

Digital reference is not simply traditional reference work without a desk. This book and the work it represents clearly demonstrates that digital reference is both expanding our understanding of traditional reference work, and incorporating ideas from fields such as business (e.g., customer support), computer science, and education. While traditional reference literature has concentrated on resources and evaluations of accuracy, digital reference is re-examining the core assumptions of reference. Traditional definitions of reference service are being redefined to incorporate new dimensions of the digital environment while other definitions are simply being discarded. It is looking at a process of reinvention where traditional norms of geography, *generalism* (assumptions that the reference librarian can serve

1

anyone's needs), and the definition of the professional are being questioned. Researchers and practitioners alike are struggling in digital reference with questions such as the democratization of the reference process (inviting subject experts into reference and referral), automation, technical infrastructure, and even the relationship between reference staff and the collection.

Reference services can be defined as mediated interfaces between users in an "anomalous state of knowledge" (Belkin, 1980) and a collection of information (Sutton, 1996: 131–33). The user's anomalous state of knowledge, also referred to as a gap in understanding (Dervin and Nilan, 1986), is often thought of as a question that needs to be answered. This question may be expressed as an e-mail request or a query to a system. The collection is a set of information in the form of documents, files, and/or knowledge (including human expertise). In digital reference, all the information that makes up an "answer" is delivered to a user electronically via the Internet.

This notion of "question" and "answer" is one of the first issues that digital reference must face. Ultimately reference is not simply someone asking a question and someone else providing an answer. It is about someone with an information problem working with someone with information skills. That is not to say that many information problems cannot be expressed as questions, or that a single question/answer interchange can't solve the problem; it merely serves to remind the reader that digital reference covers a larger domain than simple ready-reference. Oftentimes there needs to be a broader exchange of information than simply a subject area and a set of resources. *Why* someone is asking a question is often as important as *what* they are asking (Katz, 1997). The core of reference is *mediation*. In traditional library settings, this mediation is achieved through the reference interview, but other contexts employ other solutions.

Mediation can be performed either by a human expert (such as a reference librarian) or an automated interface (such as an online catalog). The primary purpose of the interface is to match the user's information need to the system's organization and capabilities (Taylor, 1968). The intermediary (once again, either automated or human) becomes the user's advocate to the system or collection. This view of reference is maintained in today's electronic reference environment (Sutton, 1996). The core question in today's emerging digital reference field is: how can organizations build and maintain reference services that mediate between a user's information need and a collection of information via the Internet?

IMPACTS OF THE INTERNET ON REFERENCE SERVICES

The literature shows significant impacts on reference services prompted by greater access to the Internet and Internet tools. These impacts include new skills needed by information specialists and reference librarians. The Internet is also expanding traditional library collections and improving location and access to reference resources (e.g., ready reference materials and pathfinders through World Wide Web sites, access to catalogs and electronic reference sources through telnet, etc.). Most significant to digital reference, the Internet affords reference services the ability to conduct entire reference transactions via the Internet, from specifying users' needs to delivering information from the collection.

A great deal of literature has focused on augmenting traditional reference services with Internet resources and capabilities. This literature ranges from evaluation criteria for online reference sources (Balas, 1995) to discussions of technology used to locate and access Internet resources (examples include Feeney, 1993; Bobp, Kratzert and Richey, 1993; Gainor and Foster, 1993; Arms, 1990; Branse, 1993; Machovec, 1993). In these discussions, the interface to the user remains the same, but the collection is expanded to include Internet resources. These new resources change the reference environment. Mardikian and Kesselman (1995: 22–23) presented five "rationales for changing reference":

- Increasing access to resources beyond the library (networked resources including the Internet).
- Lack of geographic constraints for users ("users may no longer need to come to the library to obtain information").
- The need to differentiate services to different populations of users (i.e., inside an organization and outside an organization) in the face of shrinking budgets.

- Increases in complexity of information resources and the need for specialized knowledge.
- New options (primarily in staffing) for answering reference questions.

All of these rationales concentrate on having librarians redefine their roles within a traditional, geographically defined library setting. One of the key changes in using digital resources in traditional reference is the professional relationship with the collection.

Taylor (1968) outlines a series of filters for the reference librarian to use in answering a patron's question. One of these filters is the match between the patron's question and the library collection. With the Internet and the introduction of other dynamic digital information sources, this filter must be dramatically expanded. Now, the librarian must ask, "What is the relationship between the patron's question and the dynamic information world?" The introduction of the Internet has, in essence, disconnected the reference librarian from the library collection. The well-pruned, carefully selected collection of physical resources in the library is dwarfed by the currency and broad scope of Internet resources. This makes the library collection only one possible resource.

This disconnect from a library collection has also forced the reference librarian to make selection decisions at the point of inquiry. The librarian must now decide what is a quality resource, and what resource best addresses a topic other than a subject bibliographer or collection development staff. The reference librarian has been transformed from information interface to a true information broker. Many would argue this is not a new role, but the Internet has certainly extenuated the reference librarian as independent operator. In essence, reference librarians can now perform their functions independent of physical library collections.

However, while these enormous questions remain in digital reference, the field goes well beyond the notion of answering traditional reference questions in traditional reference environments (the reference desk) with digital sources. Digital reference as a field, instead, looks at the entire reference process online.

KEY ISSUES IN DIGITAL REFERENCE

Digital issues in traditional reference have been well defined, including cost of digital resources, quality of Web resources, training of personnel, etc. On the other hand, these issues are only beginning to emerge in digital reference. Two key issues in conducting reference transactions in an Internet-only mode have already come to light. These core issues are: scalability (the ability for services to grow) and ambiguity (identifying the resources needed to meet users' needs before answering a question).

Scalability

Scalability is a term originally coined in manufacturing. The term refers to a process whereby production of an item can be increased to maximize efficiency and effectiveness. Companies would have to determine how to maximize investment so that processes and machines created as prototypes could then be either replaced, or built upon in order to make five hundred items, then one thousand, then one million, and so on. The key was to invest wisely; putting in place sufficient infrastructure to meet demand, while not bankrupting the company on hardware that would never be utilized fully. When discussing human beings, significant variables for scalability include quality of work and ethics of the profession in addition to efficiency and effectiveness.

While it may seem quite a jump from production lines to reference services, the question still remains: how can a digital reference service grow, or scale, to handle a large number of questions, given that traditional scaling mechanisms such as service hours and geographical constraints run counter to users' expectations on the Internet? This issue was faced first in non-human mediated contexts. For example, when the Library of Congress first put its catalog online (through a gopher site), it only kept the service running from 9 A.M. to 5 P.M. Internet users were confused as to why they couldn't search the catalog anytime they wanted; after all, wasn't that the point of the Internet? Internet users are used to getting information whenever they need it. This actually makes sense. Librarians have always known that reference questions do not simply occur to patrons between 9 A.M. and 5 P.M.

Yet many libraries, as they move to Internet reference services, have kept in place traditional scalability schemes from their physical counterparts. These libraries allow access to digital reference services only to patrons from a given community (through library card numbers, etc.) or restrict patrons to real-time service that functions during limited hours of the day. These restrictions of time and space made sense in physical reference environments, but go against the norms of the Internet.

Restrictions based on geographic location are at the very least problematic. It is more useful to discuss restrictions of membership. That is to say, in order to have access to a service, you must be a member of a given community that supports the library or digital reference service. It makes no sense for an academic library to answer the questions of students at other academic institutions. This could also be true of members of a geographical community supporting a public library; many would agree the service should be restricted to taxpayers. This elimination of geography for membership has implications. Academic libraries are confronting these right now. Restricting to a student body these days is no longer about place. What about distance students? You may answer the questions of students who are never physically present on a campus. Further, these students may live several time zones away. In public library contexts, what about patrons on vacation or living temporarily abroad? What about library members who work night shifts, or who simply need library service out of set hours? So by moving from a restriction of place to membership, we see that we are really moving from a restriction of time and place to a new restriction based on a library's means of support.

The restriction of time then becomes the truly problematic notion. We can indeed restrict the use (and therefore control scaling issues) by the time of day during which we offer the service. But as we have just discussed, these limitations of "hours" become increasingly arbitrary in an environment of around-the-clock work and commerce. If people can buy books, search for Websites, and even check their stocks at 2 A.M. (anywhere in the world), why can't they at least submit a question to their local library?

Current Scalability Efforts

Currently there are several approaches to overcoming the limitations of "9 to 5" reference. One is borrowed from traditional reference: extend hours. Academic, public, and even school libraries pay professionals and paraprofessionals to stay at a desk beyond normal hours. This approach incorporates real-time technologies such as chat and video conferencing to allow patrons to have access to reference professionals at a distance. It replicates the intimacy of one-to-one reference interviews and requires little retraining on the part of the reference professional (other than technical training). However, it virtually eliminates the possibility of collaborative reference services (networking the reference function beyond a single organization or incorporating experts beyond the library domain), greatly increases the resources needed by the patron to use the service, and still forces both reference staff and patrons into a potentially uncomfortable one-to-one interaction.

Another approach, typified by the Library of Congress effort, takes into account that libraries in all time zones are facing these issues. The Collaborative Digital Reference Service headed up by the Library of Congress (see Part 2) looks to network reference desks all over the world to provide after hours service. A patron in New York at 2 A.M. could talk to a reference specialist in Australia. Other library consortia are also looking into these networked services on a smaller scale. The advantage to these approaches is the use of existing resources. However, all assume excess capacity in current services. The New York user can only utilize the Australian resources at 2 A.M. if the Australian reference librarian isn't busy. While technical infrastructure and administrative details will be difficult to work out, the real question is: is there unused staff time in the current library-based reference service, and if so, will organizations be willing to share it?

Possibly the most common digital reference scalability solution in use today is *asynchronous reference*. Asynchronous reference uses either a Web page or e-mail to take a question into a service at any time, and to answer it when resources are available. Such a system allows easy networking of services and allows for scheduling of resources. However, asynchronous reference makes the assumption that users can either completely represent their queries without a reference interview or that such limitations can be overcome through iteration (a series of exchanges over time). Where real-time approaches emphasize the value of immediacy of reference, asynchronous reference emphasizes the context that reference staff can offer, even if it takes longer. There are ample examples of such approaches including many AskA services (Lankes, 1998; Wasik 1999a; Lankes and Kasowitz, 1998).

Ambiguity

Where scalability refers to services, ambiguity refers to the questions asked of services. The ability to automate and regularize, a key to scalability, assumes limited ambiguity in the questions asked. In the commercial help-desk sector, for example, companies have solved the problem of users with ambiguous information needs by limiting the domains that users can ask questions about. The classic phone menu has found a place on the Internet as a series of hierarchical menus that users must navigate before they can answer a question (with the company often hoping the user either finds the answer along the way, or simply gives up trying). By limiting the domain of the question, an organization (library or company) can limit the time and effort needed to answer the question. In library settings this can be seen in the creation of subject bibliographers, specialized "reading rooms" and other means of forcing users to limit their domain before they ever ask a question.

The new crop of information markets (Wasik, 1999b) is currently wrestling with these issues as they seek to create "reference for fee" services. How can you put a cost on answering a question before you answer that question? Certainly we have all had the experience of setting out to find a quick answer to an "easy" question and wonder what happened hours later. The library world finds the questions of ambiguity particularly trying due to its open domain and its commitment to a contextualized answer. Several initiatives are underway to build so-called reference knowledge bases or databases. It will be interesting to see how they succeed when users rarely ask the same question twice. Think of the problems with descriptive cataloging multiplied a hundred fold. Perhaps the answer to the scalability question is through a network of highly specialized (low ambiguity) reference services.

The key to handling ambiguity seems to be providing an appropriate level of interactivity. Whether real-time or asynchronous, how can digital reference services provide an opportunity for users to best express their information needs? Taylor has already argued that reference work is some of the most difficult information work in the world because users have to express something they don't know (Taylor, 1968). How can we make sure the users have every opportunity to seek help, refine their questions, and ultimately answer their questions?

PUTTING IT ALL TOGETHER

Digital reference may seem new to many. To some it may seem like reference with e-mail. It is clear, however, that digital reference is more than a simple set of techniques and technologies—it is an attempt by the library and related communities to come to terms with human intermediation in today's digital libraries. As physical libraries reinvent themselves into public access centers, and special librarians transform themselves into in-context information consultants, the reference staff must come to grips with its changing world. It is very healthy to review common sense and practice on a regular basis. It is healthy to see how our ethics and values translate into a new domain. It is healthy to seek input beyond our ranks to other domains for guidance and good ideas. Digital reference as a domain is a positive sign that reference is alive and well.

REFERENCES

Arms, Caroline R. 1990. "Using the National Networks: BITNET and the Internet." *Online* 14, no. 5 (September): 24–29.

Balas, Janet. 1995. "The Internet and Reference Services." *Computers in Libraries* 15, no. 6 (June): 39–41.

Belkin, Nicholas J. 1980. "Anomalous States of Knowledge as a Basis for Information Retrieval." *Canadian Journal of Information Science* 5 (May): 133–43.

Bobp, Mary Ellen, Mona Y. Kratzert, and Debora Richey. 1993. "The Emergence of Systemwide Electronic Access to Information Sources: The Experience of Two California State University Libraries." *The Reference Librarian* no. 39: 111–30.

Branse, Y. 1993. "Internet Resources: How Not to Get Tangled Up in the Net." *Bulletin of the Israel Society of Special Libraries and Information Centers* 19, no. 2: 21–25.

Dervin, Brenda and Michael Nilan. 1986. "Information Needs and Uses." *Annual Review of Information Science and Technology* 21: 3–31.

Feeney, Ann. 1993. "Internet Applications: STUMPERS-L." *Computers in Libraries* 13, no. 5: 40–42.

Gainor, Lawrence A. and Erin E. Foster. 1993. "Usenet and the Library." *Reference Services Review* 21, no. 3: 7–22.

Katz, William A. 1997. *Introduction to Reference Work.* Vol. 2, *Reference Services and Reference Processes.* 7th ed. New York: McGraw-Hill.

Lankes, R. David. 1998. *Building and Maintaining Internet Information Services: K–12 Digital Reference Services.* Syracuse, N.Y.: ERIC Clearinghouse on Information and Technology.

Lankes, R. David and Abby S. Kasowitz. 1998. *AskA Starter Kit: How to Build and Maintain Digital Reference Services.* Syracuse, N.Y.: ERIC Clearinghouse on Information & Technology.

Machovec, G. 1993. "VERONICA: A Gopher navigational tool on the Internet." *Online Libraries and Microcomputers* 11, no. 10: 1–4.

Mardikian, Jackie and Martin A. Kesselman. 1995. "Beyond the Desk: Enhanced Reference Staffing for the Electronic Library. *Reference Services Review* 23, no. 1: 21–28.

Sutton, S. 1996. Future Service Models and the Convergence of Functions: The Reference Librarian as Technician, Author and Consultant. In *The Roles of Reference Librarians: Today and Tomorrow,* edited by K. Low. New York: Haworth Press.

Taylor, R. 1968. "Question Negotiation and Information Seeking in Libraries." *College & Research Libraries* 29: 178–194.

Wasik, Joann M. (1999a). "Building and Maintaining Digital Reference Services." *ERIC Digest.* [Online] *http://ericir.syr.edu/ithome/digests/digiref.html* (Accessed 2 May 2000).

Wasik (1999b). "Information for Sale: Commercial Digital Reference and AskA Services." [Online] *http://www.vrd.org/AskA/commAskA.html* (Accessed 2 May 2000).

Part I

The New Reference Culture: Traits And Trends

OVERVIEW

Much of the early conversation concerning digital reference service focused on the technical aspects of designing automated systems. Indeed, many of the people developing these systems were outside of the library academy and approached the challenges of digital services from a systems perspective. Little attention was given to "person-to-person" interaction in deference to the belief that questions could efficiently and easily be answered by accessing databases.

The papers presented here examine this issue and discuss the provision of digital reference in the context of traditional library services. Collectively, the following chapters address the changing nature of reference service, the evolution of a new set of values for information service professionals, and the need for human assistance in the digital environment. The authors contend that the Internet has altered the expectations of library users and changed the service perspectives of librarians and other information providers. The changing relationship between service providers and information seekers is examined and new sets of values and beliefs are discussed.

Why Reference Is About to Change Forever (but Not Completely)

Joseph Janes

This paper examines the nature of library reference and the effect that the introduction of the connectivity of the Internet could have on it. Resources that are important to this emerging environment are discussed, including information, technologies, people, and financial resources. Steps in the adoption of innovations (automation, migration, and transformation) are summarized. Potential developments in a more highly interconnected reference world are suggested, including reusable reference objects and artifacts, use of data mining techniques, important roles for generalists and specialists, a presence in the library catalog, and new types of questions and greater depth of responses. It is concluded that the mediating presence of reference is about to evolve in a profound and exceptional way.

INTRODUCTION: HOOKING PEOPLE UP

Digital reference is on people's minds a lot these days. Many libraries are experimenting with answering reference questions via a variety of technological means or using digital resources in answering queries. Articles are being written and research is beginning to appear which describes processes, characteristics of services, and so on (Abels, 1996; Lipow, 1997; Tenopir and Ennis, 1998; Lagace, 1999; Janes and McClure, 1999). It's probably a platitude by now to say that digital reference, in all its various guises, will happen and will be part of the set of techniques used by reference librarians in their future work.

But what, then, will happen to "reference"? Beyond the technical questions of setting up a service or conducting training sessions to help staff use networked resources in doing reference, there are deeper questions to be asked about the very nature of reference itself, and the effect that the introduction of Internet connectivity has on it. These are, to be sure, speculations, but they might be helpful in thinking about what may be possible or desirable as we move forward.

First, a more general question: What happens when people get connected? They can:

- Start to communicate, probably more than they did before, and perhaps more effectively as they get to know each other;
- Share information, experiences, and ideas;
- Begin to become interdependent, as sharing leads to reliance;
- Build up mutual understanding, knowledge, and trust; and
- Build a community and grow stronger through their interconnection.

To be sure, this isn't always the case, and history is full of examples of people and groups who had plenty of connection and hated each other. But since we're talking about librarians here, the above scenario seems more plausible, not to mention more pleasant.

The library world is full of examples of such interconnection and interdependence. Probably the best example is OCLC; it's hard to imagine the library world today without it, and it's hard to imagine how individual libraries would function without some sort of collaborative cataloging and interlibrary loan (ILL) venture. ILL is another example of sharing and interdependence based on interconnection, as is the reference question listserv STUMPERS-L, and the cooperative reference services of earlier days that are its ancestors. Many libraries of all types are members of consortia, networks and systems, which provide centralized services and are becoming increasingly important in this day of licensed databases and intricate vendor negotiations.

And all of these examples of interconnection and interdependence are the result of our being poor. Let's face the truth—if libraries as a group were better funded and supported, it's quite likely that some of these examples of sharing would not exist or be far less extensive. None of this should be interpreted as criticism (other than our lack of ability to engender fuller support from our user populations); indeed, the degree of creativity and ingenuity demonstrated here, not to mention willingness to work together, are to be marveled at and should be a great source of pride for the library world.

The preceding discussion is relevant because the environment in which reference is conducted is changing, becoming more interconnected and perhaps interdependent. If that is the case, then the implications of that environment bear further scrutiny and creative thought. There are several sets of resources that will be important in this emerging environment, each of which is discussed below.

RESOURCES

Information

Of course, this is the basis of reference: a set of information resources, which can be searched to find the one(s) most appropriate for a person's information need. In the past, these resources would largely (although not exclusively) have been in print form and would have to be owned and physically held by a library to be useful, not to mention actually there, undamaged, up-to-date, etc. Technological advancements such as the telephone have broken down some, but not all, of those barriers.

The Internet has changed all that. Now we can use those valuable resources as well as much more global ones: resources that may or may not be freely available; may be licensed by the vendor, publisher or even the author; and may be only available at a given time, for a given amount of time, or on an on-demand, by-the-drink basis. The nature of information resources is changing and will continue to change as technology changes, but also as people change, the economy changes, societies change, and so on. This is not a new phenomenon, to be sure;

information resources have been evolving continually since the development of writing, but the speed and nature of change have accelerated greatly.

Technologies

Quite apart from the information resources they can convey, the raw technologies are changing as well. Computing and telecommunications technology is getting more powerful, faster, capable of handling and delivering more bandwidth and dropping in price (for the same capability), and will continue to do so for at least the near future.

In addition, new kinds of hardware will be important to the reference world, including cell phones and headsets (so useful for roaming the stacks while on the phone with a patron) and small personal digital information appliances (e.g., the current Palm Pilot and its more powerful and more useful successors). These appliances will also have wireless network connections to allow Web browsing and other Internet activity while doing other remote tasks.

Software is also evolving. Reference should take notice of videoconferencing applications (e.g., NetMeeting, CU-SeeMe), instant messaging (e.g., ICQ, AOL), autosearching (e.g., Ask Jeeves), new information formats (e.g., MP3), data mining (the analysis of data for relationships not previously discovered), chatterbots (program that attempts to simulate human conversation), and so on.

In short, we are entering a world where technology can enable us to have much more interaction with people than is currently possible. This interaction will be different in important ways, but as with mail and phone and teletype, reference should embrace, explore and exploit these technologies as appropriate (Ryan, 1996).

People

Many, if not most, librarians are familiar and comfortable with the notion of people as resources to use in the reference process: they ask questions of colleagues, they refer patrons to other agencies or services, and they even sometimes answer questions based on their own personal knowledge or opinion.

The kind of interconnection we have available now, though, makes possible greater and wider use of such people-as-resources. The large and growing number of ask-an-expert services, where people, groups, and organizations are providing answers to questions in their areas of expertise, can be of tremendous value. They proceed from different premises than do reference librarians. Many of them have no "information" training, so they tend to answer questions rather than instruct people on information use or evaluations, and they often won't answer or respond to questions outside their areas of expertise. However, these are not necessarily shortcomings. These services, and the people behind them, are in the same basic business as reference librarians, and they could be valuable partners, used appropriately.

Beyond these, there are literally thousands upon thousands of groups taking advantage of networked technologies to connect and communicate with each other. The Usenet groups and listservs of the mid- and late 1990s are now complemented with Web rings, Yahoo! clubs, and Onelist groups, not to mention chatrooms, eBay's café, and message boards. These groups, since their very basis for existence depends on the sharing of information on common interests, could also be of tremendous use as sources of assistance in the reference endeavor with appropriate evaluation and discretion.

But if these groups are out there, what is the role of the reference librarian? Well, it's pretty much what it always was—working with people to determine the nature of their information needs, identifying potentially valuable sources of information to help them satisfy their needs, evaluating those sources, and presenting them in a useful way.

In addition, there has been a continuing discussion for many years about the nature of librarianship. Are librarians better off as *specialists*, being extremely well versed in a particular subject area, or as *generalists*, able to be conversant if not expert in many (or all) fields to help people take the right next steps? This is an insoluble debate, and both seem to coexist, although librarians in one-person libraries, highly specialized research institutes or subject-specific institutions have answers of their own by necessity.

Financial

This, as the saying goes, is the $64,000 question. (Or perhaps, today, the $1,000,000 question. $64,000 doesn't go as far as it used to.) We all know which direction budgets are going, and there's a pervasive (but so far anecdotal and unresearched) notion that fewer people are asking questions of reference desks because they are finding information much more easily than they used to on the Internet. There are plenty of other possible explanations for this, but reasons notwithstanding, if reference question numbers fall, there will be even greater budgetary pressure on reference departments, not to mention the increased commitments to expensive licensed resources. Consortia and networks will help, but in planning any sort of cooperative reference enterprise, the question will quite rightly be asked by administrators, governing boards, and communities: Why are we spending precious resources to answer questions for people who aren't contributing to our library?

It's a valid question and an important one. The pattern has been set by OCLC, interlibrary loan, and other cooperative services to which many contribute for mutual benefit (not unlike libraries themselves, of course). More pivotally, though, this goes to the question of the *scalability* of the reference enterprise. Can the kind of individually based, handcrafted service we have come to expect in "reference" survive in a world of millions of questions per day?

ADOPTION OF INNOVATIONS

Step One: Automation

The first step in the process of introducing technology to an existing system is usually automation. We saw this in the first generation of online catalogs. (Remember those early systems, which displayed the catalog information exactly as it would have appeared on the card, down to the dot at the bottom, which was where the rod would have gone through the card?) We're in that stage now with digital reference. People are simply moving their traditional reference services into the digital world, taking reference questions via e-mail, answering them via e-mail (or even by phone in some cases), using networked resources to answer questions, and so on. This is fine, and to be expected, but it by no means takes full advantage of the technologies and other resources out there.

Step Two: Migration

Once people get used to a technological environment, they learn more about how to take fuller advantage. Current catalog systems, with integrated library catalogs, databases, Websites, and assistance are examples of this phenomenon. In the digital reference world, this might involve passing questions around among services, sharing resources, taking advantage of the expertise of known (and perhaps unknown) partners in a network.

This would be a set of new models of practice, not predicated on a single, fairly static collection of resources, but on a more fluid set. Resources would include people, organizations, and other services (run by libraries and not other parties), using a wide range of technologies as appropriate. Librarians who are entering the profession now are starting out thinking of the Internet as just another set of tools, and the way they do reference and the services they will help to develop and refine will be based on this assumption.

Here's another take on the specialist vs. generalist discussion. If we envision a collaborative service, taking advantage of many different institutions, services, collections, and sets of staff, perhaps there are meaningful roles to be played by both. Generalists could take the first crack at incoming questions, either responding to them directly if they're ready-reference type queries, or forwarding them to the appropriate second-level (read "specialist") staff for further work. These specialists could then either, again, answer the question directly, or go yet further, calling on experts and communities to assist, perhaps also introducing inquirers to groups and services they did not know exist but wish to be part of. This results not only in answer of a particular question but in reinforcing the group and enhancing the person's life in ways we couldn't understand initially.

Step Three: Transformation

And then what? With luck, the next stage will be something entirely different, the shape and nature of which is difficult if not impossible to predict. Instead of sharing and cooperating because we have to (due to poverty), we can build sharing and cooperative systems because we can, due to opportunity.

WHAT MIGHT HAPPEN

Here are a few ideas, most of which probably won't come to pass, but which might at least serve to give some notions of what could be possible in a more highly interconnected and networked world.

Imagine reference in a world with:

1. *Reusable reference objects and artifacts*
   Every reference inquiry is captured in some form, along with the process that is used to respond to it, the results as presented to the user, and feedback from the user on the usefulness, relevance, and their satisfaction with the response. These "reference objects" are then stored for evaluation of services, and reused for similar or identical subsequent inquiries.

2. *The use of data mining techniques*
   Standard database or information retrieval techniques would be somewhat useful on repositories of these objects, but data mining would be even more valuable, allowing identification of patterns, associations, and clusters of similar or related questions and answers, including those we might not otherwise find.

3. *Important roles for generalists and specialists*
   A cadre of generalist, triage librarians scan each incoming inquiry, answering those they can with ready-refer-

ence resources, and quick searches using the reference object repository, or AskJeeves-like search mechanisms. More involved inquiries are forwarded to specialist librarians with access to extensive specialized resources, including experts, communities and groups, advanced data mining tools, and technologies to assist in semi-automated interviews with patrons (via chat, live video links, e-mail, or Internet telephony, as appropriate). These specialist librarians number in the thousands and have expertise in sometimes quite small domains, maintaining their own collections of resources (available via the Internet to others), which are organized, evaluated, and easy to use and find.

4. *A presence in the library's catalog*
   To be useful, reference services have to be where people are. This means at the desk and on the phone, but also in the stacks and hallways, on e-mail, and in the catalog. Catalog systems include links to direct help ("Click here to ask a real librarian for help!"), leading users into the reference system in a seamless and painless way using video, audio, and screen control technologies. In addition, links to frequently asked questions (FAQs as we now know them, in addition to reference objects from the repository), experts, and other services are available.

5. *New types of questions, greater depth of responses*
   As Internet tools of all types become easier to use and more resources become available, ready-reference questions continue to dwindle, in favor of more in-depth and detailed inquiries. As the amount of information swells, people increasingly seek advice on what not to look at or read, and guidance services, built on readers' advisory and other familiar functions of librarianship, arise to help people focus their increasingly scarce attention on the most important and valuable resources.

Underlying all of this would be the emergence of a body of knowledge about reference in this environment: how to do it, who does what well (experts, specialized librarians, collections—perhaps librarians will even compete to offer service in subject areas), object repositories that include the best paths, strategies and responses, and evaluations of human and informational resources.

An economy might arise, like that around interlibrary loan or cooperative cataloging. Some libraries and librarians might be Net answerers, others Net questioners, but all will participate for the greater good of all patrons. Governing boards and the public are pleased with the increasing level of service to meet new demands and outreach to new communities both geographic and otherwise. The use of experts and communities also could go a long way in addressing the scalability question; correctly and appropriately used, they can be the "extra" resources necessary to allow the reference enterprise to scale beyond its current capacity.

At some point, the whole becomes more than the sum of its parts, and we move beyond just question-answering to something more complete, more involved, and more satisfying, to both inquirers and ourselves. We should use these technologies and other resources to strive toward the full realization of what we have always wanted to do—enable people to get what they want and need to help them move through their lives.

For several thousand years, since our collective knowledge was recorded and no longer shared from person to person, it has been imprisoned in physical containers; these are safe, secure, and preserved but often hard to find, lost, or invisible. This newest set of technologies can break open those barriers.

When information is in physical form, and you want to maintain a central repository for many people to use, you have to have somewhere to put it. The idea of amassing collections and maintaining those repositories is called a "library"; that idea was for so long required to have a place, that the place became confused with the idea.

The "library" isn't the building, fetching and attractive as that notion is to librarians and users. The "library" is the *idea behind the building* and what goes on inside. Now that the information and knowledge contained there no longer have to be *in* that building, the idea can be extended to where it belongs and is most needed. Physical materials (print, but also sound recordings, images, microforms, cuneiform, papyri, etc.) will always be with us. The buildings will always be necessary and will have continuing and requisite value as community meeting places and venues for access to resources of all formats by people not able to afford them on their own. But that's not all there is any more.

Libraries, then, to truly serve their users in the best possible way, have to *be somewhere and everywhere.* Reference services must then do likewise.

We have libraries to share, preserve, collect, represent, and provide access to the record of the human condition. We have libraries for cultural survival and propagation; a society, which cannot transmit itself to future generations, dies very quickly and will be unmourned. We have libraries because, as a species, we're better off with them than we would be without, and civilizations for thousands of years and all around the world have understood that. Reference, for the last hundred years or so, has made libraries work and will continue to do so, because it will always be hard to find stuff (especially the right, best stuff). That mediating presence is about to evolve in a profound and exceptional way.

Or at least it better.

REFERENCES

Abels, Eileen. 1996. "The E-mail Reference Interview." *RQ* 36, no.3 (Spring): 345–58.

Janes, Joseph and Charles R. McClure. 1999. "The Web as a Reference Tool Comparisons with Traditional Sources." *Public Libraries* 38, no. 1 (January/February): 30–39.

Lagace, Nettie. 1999. Establishing Online Reference Services. Pp. 153–84 in *The Internet Public Library Handbook,* edited by Joseph Janes, David Carter, Annette Lagace, Michael McLennen, Sara Ryan, and Schelle Simcox. New York: Neal-Schuman.

Lipow, Anne Grodzins. 1997. "Thinking Out Loud: Who Will Give Reference Service in the Digital Environment?" *Reference & User Services Quarterly* 37, no. 2 (Winter): 125–29.

Ryan, Sara. 1996. "Reference Service for the Internet Community: A Case Study of the Internet Public Library Reference Division." *Library & Information Science Research* 18, no. 3 (Summer): 241–59.

Tenopir, Carol and Lisa Ennis. 1998. "The Digital Reference World of Academic Libraries." *Online* 22 (July/August): 22–28.

Transforming Reference Staffing for the Digital Library

Susan Lessick

This paper discusses the need for academic librarians to redefine current staffing systems in order to accommodate digital reference service and describes three digital reference initiatives at the University of California, Irvine (UCI) Libraries—video reference, Web reference, and call messaging. Topics include evolving reference staffing trends; the impact of networking on reference service; future network reference services; and staffing strategies for the digital library.

INTRODUCTION

The digital library offers users the prospect of remote, around-the-clock access to electronic resources. Most academic librarians define and view the digital library solely in terms of resources and content. This paper suggests that academic librarians need to rethink that concept. As a number of librarians have so convincingly pointed out in recent publications, there is a serious need for bringing service perspectives and traditions of the physical library to the digital library (Ferguson and Bunge, 1997; Sloan, 1998; Tennant, 1999). Human assistance in the digital environment is badly needed, as users lack the most basic skills in using Web-based catalogs, indexes, circulation, reserves, and ILL systems, search engines, and databases. This new digital service environment requires that we radically change our perspectives on user needs and transform the ways in which we organize roles of reference staff to serve these needs.

UCI LIBRARIES DIGITAL SERVICE INITIATIVES

Over the past three years, University of California, Irvine (UCI) Libraries have initiated three digital service delivery methods that employ technology to extend reference assistance to public workstations throughout the library and to our remote users. These initiatives have enhanced UCI student and faculty access to online support while using digital materials.

Video Reference Project

Since 1996, science librarians at UCI have been actively testing the use of real-time videoconferencing to provide online reference support to student users at various remote locations. In 1997, the science librarians used a live video connection between the science reference desk and a College of Medicine computer lab located one-half mile away to provide real-time reference assistance to medical students in that lab. Video reference service was offered for one hour a day, Monday through Friday, for two quarters of the academic year. Since then, the science librarians have tested various applications and equipment at different on- and off-campus locations. Based on these experiences and the continuous improvement of desktop videoconferencing technology and the UCI campus telecommunication infrastructure, a small team of librarians is now planning to offer daily video reference service to a medical branch library located 13 miles from campus by fall quarter 2000.

Web Reference Project

In fall 1999, we launched a new centralized, team-based Web reference service with a specific link from the library's home page. Student and faculty use of the new service has increased since that time and in several recent surveys, users indicate that they are pleased with the quick responses and the convenience of use. An evaluation of this project is featured in the paper "Evaluating the 'Ask a Question' Service at the University of California, Irvine," by Judy Horn and Kathryn Kjaer, found in Part 5 of this text.

Call Messaging Project

The third digital service that we have recently implemented is called the Reference Call Messaging Project. The reference areas in the two large on-campus libraries are currently testing a new call-button messaging system on the public PCs and on the reference desk workstations. This project uses a network application to exchange messages between users working at the public PCs and the reference staff working at the reference desk. The project involves placing an icon on each of the public workstations that says, "Click Here to Call a Librarian." When users need assistance at these workstations, they now have the capability of "calling" a librarian from their desktop computer. After the user clicks the icon, a window appears on the user's screen that says a librarian will be available shortly. This message is also sent over the network to the reference desk workstation. A window and audio prompt on the reference desk workstation then alerts the librarian that the user needs help and indicates which public computer called for assistance. This project allows users to remain at their workstations along with their work and belongings while seeking assistance elsewhere. This service was implemented for two months this summer in both campus library locations. The pilot only recently ended and is now being evaluated.

EVOLVING MODELS FOR REFERENCE SERVICE

New digital service alternatives that meet emerging needs are compelling reference librarians to analyze their operations in order to get a more systemic view of services so that effective staffing configurations can be developed. They will require new staffing models to bring together the continued use of traditional, on-site reference while affording a flexible and gradual adaptation to new electronic reference delivery methods.

Before discussing digital service models and their various staffing strategies, this section will present some of the more recent "progressive" reference trends that have been widely discussed in the library literature. It is helpful to examine these trends, because it seems that new digital service models are extensions of these ongoing trends that first appeared in the "re-thinking reference" literature in the 1980s.

Some of the more common "progressive" reference approaches that are frequently mentioned are:

- tiered service
- roving librarians
- growth of research consultation activities
- increasing number of librarians actually working outside of the library in the academic departments and even maintaining office hours in departments
- use of more paraprofessionals and students in reference.

Overlaid on these evolving models of reference is the fact that the computer network has had a transforming and revolutionary impact on academic librarianship (Ferguson and Bunge, 1997). The proliferation of digital resources, networks, and various enabling technologies have, and will continue to, transform all of the services the library offers to users. Witness the increase of Web-based catalogs, circulation, reserve and ILL systems, and gateway library Websites.

IMPACT OF NETWORKING ON REFERENCE SERVICE

We are also witnessing the ways that the digital environment is impacting and reshaping reference.

Reference Sources

Until the last few years, reference desk librarians worked exclusively with carefully selected site-based print sources. Today, reference desk librarians are increasingly using information sources on the Web that provide a tremendous array of source material. This large universe of information presents many challenges for the reference librarian such as locating high-quality information sources and educating users about the need to critically evaluate Web sources.

Technical Support

The expansion in the number and complexity of information resources and in the means for accessing and manipulating them
has brought renewed attention to user needs for technical or
mechanical assistance. Today, reference librarians routinely provide technical assistance to users who have hardware, software,
and networking problems.

New Digital Reference Services

Another impact is that academic libraries are beginning to offer reference service via e-mail and electronic form from library
Websites. Some are even exploring the use of synchronous
online support services over the network and the feasibility and
benefits of participating in cooperative digital services.

Development of Web-based Resources and Tools

Another important impact of networks on reference is that librarians are actively developing electronic research guides, interface systems, and user-directed interactive educational programs on the selection and use of library resources. These self-
help online tools give users needed information and skills at all
times and from all locations. One superb example of these new
user-directed tools is the Research QuickStart service at the University of Minnesota that provides electronic research guides to
users (primarily undergraduates) on a broad range of research
topics (*http://research.lib.umn.edu*).

Another example, Database Advisor, was developed at the
University of California at San Diego (*http://scilib.ucsd.edu/Proj/
dba/*). This interface helps users select the appropriate databases
for their topic based on the number of retrieved citations on that
topic in each database. Finally, librarians at the University of
Texas System Digital Library developed an interactive information literacy program called TILT (*http://tilt.lib.utsystem.edu/*).

FUTURE NETWORK OF REFERENCE SERVICES

Based on our experience at Irvine and other digital service developments, it is the author's view that future reference services will involve a blend of approaches that will vary depending on the local environment and user needs. Reference services will encompass a mix of interrelated, complementary functions. Personal assistance to users at a physical desk will be only one component of a network of reference services we offer to users. Simmons-Welburn described this future model very well, stating that the new reality for reference will be "an organizational network of services . . . [that] can accommodate consultation, on-demand assistance, and instruction as different, yet highly compatible nodes that are themselves distinctive yet responsive to one another" (Simmons-Welburn, 1993: 61).

On-Demand Assistance

This multilayered and integrated network of reference services will include on-demand assistance. Basic informational services, ready reference assistance, technical assistance, and even advanced searching assistance offered at a physical desk on a drop-in basis, will still be needed in academic libraries to help the numerous and diverse users who continue to have information and learning needs within the library. At Irvine, we have experienced significant drops in the numbers of desk contacts. This is consistent with a national trend of declining use of reference service by users in the library. We think this decline is due to users being able to invoke resources and systems remotely and in a more independent fashion. Some evidence of this is the fact that we are seeing an explosive growth in the use of our Website. Several library sites at UCI are some of the most heavily used sites on campus. At the same time, however, librarians at the desk report that users need more complicated assistance and that the questions they ask require more time to answer. We plan to study this situation more closely in our next user survey of reference and document the complexity of reference questions asked by looking at the number of library assistant referrals, time involved in completing transactions, and the number of resources used to answer questions. So, until the number of on-site users diminishes dramatically, on-demand assistance for users in the library at the desk will need to continue.

Besides desk service, on-site assistance for users will also include receiving help at their public workstations. This could take the form of a call messaging system, as described earlier, or online chat tools available on the user's desktop to communicate with the attendant or reference librarian at the desk from remote locations within the library. In this way, the physical desk would serve as a "virtual" desk for the users at public PCs within the library. Users could message or chat with library staff at the desk to get immediate assistance or to report problems.

Research Consultation

Research consultation by referral or by appointment will also be an important component of future reference service. Personal consultation provides an effective means for users to obtain more in-depth assistance or instruction that could not be otherwise obtained in a quick interchange at the reference desk. Users should have the opportunity to make appointments with a librarian to discuss a research issue at the desk, over the phone, or by electronic form on the library's Website. Consultation service should be viewed as an integral part of desk service as it is an effective way to redirect and off-load complex or lengthy transactions from the desk to reference professionals who can work with the user collaboratively and take the needed time to answer more complex questions. Consultation service should be offered both by appointment and on a drop-in basis. Drop-in consultation service should be scheduled to coordinate with the hours of heaviest use on the desk.

In the future, consultations by appointment in the digital environment will also be feasible. Videoconferencing and collaboration technology provide effective means of interacting with remote users. The video service worked best at Irvine when users made 30-minute appointments to speak to a librarian at the Science Library about a research need or search problem for extended periods of time.

New Digital Reference Services

Increasingly, digital reference service will be an important element in the array of reference services provided by academic libraries. Librarians and support staff will be expected to answer questions and provide instruction to users asynchronously by electronic mail and Web form from the library's Website. Users will also expect that digital service be available 24 hours a day. Additionally, users will expect to have synchronous online support services similar to services that are now available in the e-commerce environment. Collaboration tools and video-conferencing will commonly be used to deliver a full range of reference services, technical assistance, individual consultations, and instruction.

STAFFING STRATEGIES FOR THE DIGITAL LIBRARY

Desk Staffing

Desk staffing can and should be done in such a way as to incorporate a tiered approach. Paraprofessionals should provide triage and basic information services and to make referrals to individual subject specialists who are either at the desk or on-call, or directly to a research consultation service. Students and technical assistants also should be available to provide technical support when users experience hardware, software, or networking problems or need assistance with a variety of applications. In other words, staffing configurations using library and student assistants should be stressed in desk coverage so to allow the professionals on the desk or on-call to deal with complex or lengthy questions. Supplementing desk staffing with paraprofessionals and students also has the added benefit of reducing the numbers of librarians that are needed to cover the desk so that they can redirect their efforts to provide in-depth reference, consultation, and instruction, and develop self-help information resources, among other higher-level tasks. In addition, an essential element of a tiered reference infrastructure is the development and implementation of a comprehensive ongoing reference assistant training program such as the program developed at UC Irvine (*http://sun3.lib.uci.edu/~riadm/ DEPTTEAM/rat.htm*).

Multiple tiered levels of service can occur at one centralized service point or at multiple tiered service points in the library. The author believes that one centralized service is optimal. Not only does one desk offer one-stop shopping for users, one desk also has mechanisms for immediately meeting a wide range of user needs while maximizing staffing resources. Additionally, one desk with multiple levels of staffing can best accommodate the possibility of handling various call center functions such as phone service, communicating to users via network chat tools and responding to user requests at user workstations.

Research Consultation Service

Research consultation service should be viewed as an extension of and complement to desk services. The emphasis should be to schedule librarians in a focused way that meets most user needs. This would mean scheduling consultation service in conjunction with the periods of heavy usage at the reference desk, during certain times in the academic year, etc. Some libraries have merged high-level reference assistance with research consultation by scheduling additional librarians at the desk who could provide consultation sessions as the need arises. In the future, UCI Libraries will conduct consultation sessions over the network using video or other collaboration technology at remote workstations at prearranged times.

Digital Services

Providing digital services will become a core service function in academic libraries. Digital services will require librarians to acquire additional knowledge and to learn new skills, and they will require additional time to provide, at least in the beginning. Additionally, librarians will also have to contend with different and faster service expectations in the digital environment. Given the fiscal and staffing constraints of libraries, some staffing adjustments will be necessary in the immediate future to accommodate not only this important emerging need, but also to maintain the other important core services described above. Again, the efficient use of professional staff on the desk and the minimal involvement of librarians for lower-level tasks can free up some additional time for librarians to devote to digital services. At Irvine, a team of professionals and paraprofessionals currently manages the centralized Web-based service. The current workload of the service is distributed among a team of six members and is in addition to their normal reference and consultation workloads. Shortly, however, each team member will be including hours worked on digital services in the overall complement of reference hours that each librarian is expected to work on reference tasks.

It will be very important to identify creative staffing strategies to support digital services as these services expand. Digital services could be offered in some cases instead of physical desk service when the scheduling of the desk is problematic such as weeknights, weekends, during intercessions, etc. Digital services could even be offered as a substitute to desk service when desk service is not available or feasible such as in library branch locations. Creating staffing efficiencies and providing specialized reference assistance can also be achieved by collaborating with other digital service providers; coverage of digital services could be shared and distributed among a number of participating libraries. Cooperative digital reference service could also expand the range of expert assistance that is available to local users. Other options, once services have been well established, include designating or recruiting a digital reference services librarian with requisite reference and technology skills who can further develop and maintain the service. In the long run, digital services may provide opportunities for enhancing the quality of reference service with the same or even reduced levels of staffing support. Coffman and Saxton (1999) have suggested recently that networked reference services (using a call center model for handling questions) have the potential of improving productivity and reconfiguring the types of staff used to answer reference questions.

CONCLUSION

Digital reference can be viewed as a logical extension of developments that began in the late 1980s and a continuation of trends to leverage limited resources and extend librarian expertise, resources, and services beyond the reference desk. Only now it is through the use of networking so that users can invoke library systems, resources, and assistance precisely when and where they are needed.

Future services, as well as staffing strategies will be diverse, differentiated, distributed, computer-assisted, and interrelated. Both human and nonintermediated assistance will be needed in the digital library to meet the diverse needs of users. Some users, whether because of inclination or learning style, will prefer and want human help even more than online help. In addition, librarians will still be called upon to provide assistance when users become stymied while searching for information. Other users will prefer to use computer systems without assistance. All users will benefit from having seamless and convenient access to online guides, help-screens, well-designed interfaces, and user-directed resources.

Finally, all of the various digital service initiatives presented at the 1999 VRD Digital Reference Conference and discussed in this book—including e-commerce developments, the LC initiative, AskA service developments, synchronous and call center technologies—underscore a very important notion. The reference service function that has been undervalued for the past several years, and virtually absent from the digital library in academic libraries until recently, is alive and well at the turn of the millennium. The long-standing philosophical basis for reference, individual point-of-use consultation and instruction, will continue to have a vitality and resonance into the 21st century, whether reference occurs through the Web, e-mail, video, or a physical reference desk.

REFERENCES

Coffman, Steve and Matthew L. Saxton. 1999. "Staffing the Reference Desk in the Largely-Digital Library." *The Reference Librarian* 66: 141–61.

Ferguson, Chris D. and Charles A. Bunge. 1997. "The Shape of Services to Come: Values-Based Reference Service for the Largely Digital Library." *College & Research Libraries* 58 (May): 252–65.

Simmons-Welburn, Janice. 1993. From Vision to Reality: Change at the University of Iowa. In *Rethinking Reference in Academic Libraries*, edited by Anne G. Lipow. Berkeley, Calif.: Library Solutions Press.

Sloan, Bernie. 1998. "Service Perspectives for the Digital Library Remote Reference Services." *Library Trends* 47 (Summer): 117–43.

Tennant, Roy. 1999. "Of Human and Humane Assistance." *Library Journal* 124, no. 11 (15 June): 30, 34.

Definitions of Personal Assistance in the New Millennium: Philosophical Explorations of Virtual Reference Service

Lorna Peterson

This paper questions whether values and behaviors of traditional reference librarians will continue in digital reference environments. It explores social and philosophical developments of reference service in North America with attention given to the significance of the new model of virtual reference provision. Topics include behavioral performance standards for reference service, digital reference services and human computer interaction, possible influences of technology on reference service, and impacts of digital reference on the library profession.

INTRODUCTION

Reference service has been defined as the personal assistance provided by librarians to individual library users to meet their information needs (Rothstein, 1954: 6). One activity that has been synonymous with reference service is desk duty, the scheduled period at a desk, 10–14 hours per week, to answer patrons' questions on demand. This service developed from occasional aid to scheduled assistance as libraries evolved from private to community libraries during the nineteenth century and early part of the twentieth century. More recent technological change has allowed for a broadening notion of personal assistance that is no longer face-to-face but can be also machine-mediated. However, reference service has at its core nineteenth century ideals of the helpful, friendly, approachable, professional person educated in the ways of bibliography to assist users face-to-face in their desires for information. Samuel Green of the Worcester Free Public Library is often credited with articulating reference service philosophy in 1876 as:

> When scholars and persons of high social position come to a library, they have confidence enough, in regard to the cordiality of their reception, to make known their wishes without timidity or reserve. Modest men in the humbler walks of life, and well-trained boys and girls, need encouragement before they become ready to say freely what they want. A hearty reception by a sympathizing friend, and the recognition of some one at hand who will listen to inquires, even although he may consider them unimportant, make it easy for such persons to ask questions, and put them at once on a home footing. (P. 74)

These attributes of warmth, sensitivity, and friendliness are taught to librarians through encouragement of behaviors including smiling, eye contact, nodding, and other interpersonal relationship skills (Jennerich and Jennerich, 1997). Will modern reference service values and behaviors maintain the attributes of warmth, sensitivity, and friendliness in the machine-mediated environment? This paper will look at some of the social and philosophical developments of reference service in North America with attention given to the significance of the new model of virtual reference provision. The paper presents legacies, discusses the Virtual Reference Desk Project and human computer interaction, describes influences, and ends with speculation on emerging values for modern librarianship.

LEGACIES

The reference interview has a firm tradition in modern librarianship with librarians writing about the patron-librarian conversation in the early part of the twentieth century (Jennerich and Jennerich, 1997), to the establishment of reference evaluation guidelines that incorporate behavioral performance standards (ALA, 1996). In 1996, the Reference and Adult Services Division of the American Library Association approved guidelines for training and evaluation of reference services. Successful reference transactions were determined to be assisted by these observable behaviors: approachability, interest, listening/inquiring, searching, and follow-up activities (ALA, 1996: 1–5). Aware of the challenge in serving remote users, its introduction states that some of the behavior measures will need to be adapted (ALA, 1996: 2). Previous to widespread computerization and concern for the remote user, there was another technological advance that tested librarian personal assistance: the telephone.

In a survey of librarian opinion regarding developments in public library reference services from 1932 to 1957, librarians commented on the increased use of the telephone for reference transactions and its interference with assisting on-site patrons (Phelps, 1957). Individual reference departments developed policies for aiding telephone patrons and also built in scheduled telephone reference hours in addition to scheduled desk duty (Bopp, 1995). Telephone reference serves to show that with each technological advance, librarians easily embrace technology to best serve users in an efficient and helpful manner.

THE VIRTUAL REFERENCE DESK PROJECT

The Virtual Reference Desk Project (VRD) seeks to study, support, and improve current K–12 digital reference services as well as build a foundation for a national cooperative digital reference service (Lankes, 1998: 1). For the purposes of this paper, virtual reference desk (vrd) will not just refer to the specific project noted as VRD, but also to those institutions (higher education, public libraries, etc.) that are participating in virtual reference services. The definition used here also assumes that vrds operate using human computer interaction and not an expert system approach that automates human knowledge (Lankes, 1998: 1–2). This is an important distinction, for the emphasis on synchronous, personal human interaction, in the context of librarian personal assistance values, presupposes the attributes of warmth, approachability, sensitivity, and friendliness in the conduct of reference transactions. Sloan (1997) cites several studies that consider the importance of human interaction in the digital library environment. The VRD has established the following facets for conducting quality digital reference service: accessibility, defined as easily reachable and navigable by any Internet user and achieved by designing Web interfaces that accommodate low-level machinery; prompt turnaround, defined as two business days to two weeks for answering; setting user expectations, defined as communicating at the start what it is the user will receive; interactive, defined by allowing Web-based forms and chat rooms for users to refine vague or complex queries; instructive, defined by providing directions for how a search was conducted and a path to additional resources; authoritative, that the answerer has the necessary expertise; private, that communication shall be held in confidence; reviewed, that services will be evaluated; and unbiased (Lankes and Kasowitz, 1998: 24–26).

Vrd projects are also concerned with the issue of warmth in the machine-mediated environment and delineate other challenges and solutions. Some AskA services encourage their experts to greet question posers by name. Weissman (1998: 131–33) notes that the answerer of virtual questions must beware that the poser may not have English as his/her first language, that sometimes a question must be declined, e-mail does get lost or misdirected, the information specialist is vulnerable to rudeness (due to questions inappropriate to the collection, repeat questions, etc.), and therefore must be able to compose neutral answers.

INFLUENCES

Why are librarians experimenting with this service? Industry tends to automate in order to save on personnel costs. Automated telephone services are used to replace human receptionists and thereby save money for the company (Kessler, 1996; Lubove, 1997; Michals, 1997). Customer satisfaction with automated telephone systems remains low and although some companies are willing to restore the use of human customer service representatives, the cost benefit for industry makes it likely that more services will be automated and customers will have to accept this automation (Mangelsdorf, 1995).

Libraries do not automate for cost reasons. In times of budget constraints for libraries, personnel is rarely touched; budget savings come by decreasing service hours, freezing book and serial acquisitions, and perhaps retrenching personnel lines through attrition (retirements, resignations, etc.). Librarians embrace technology and offer services to show that they are on the cutting edge to raise the profile of the library and catch the attention of those who are responsible for its fiscal health—administrators, legislators, and members of boards. Sometimes the use of technology in development of a service predates its feasibility. For example, Sloan cites lackluster results of the University of Michigan Shapiro Undergraduate Library reference experiment with desktop video conferencing technologies and CU-SeeMe software and the mixed success of the University of California, Irvine Science Library video conference experiment. In the case of Michigan, the software and equipment were not at quality development stage; in addition, there was a lack of needed technical support. At Irvine, the conditioning of students that they would not have to go to the library to ask questions was frustrated by students needing to go to the library to retrieve materials, which they did not want to do (Sloan, 1997). These examples are not presented to suggest that librarians should not experiment with technology; they are presented to illustrate that technology, always costly, may not deliver on its promises or may condition for unforeseen user expectations that create additional service challenges for librarians.

IMPACT OF DIGITAL REFERENCE ON THE PROFESSION

The development and nurturing of vrds has seen the profession engage in a spirited philosophical debate (Ferguson and Bunge, 1997; Tyckoson, 1999). With prescience, Rose Phelps noted in 1957:

> An event which will probably seem of very great significance is the advent of the electronic machine for storage

and retrieval of information. Evidently it can greatly facilitate the production of wonderful new reference tools, . . .
but if it should destroy the personal relationship between
reader and librarian and if it should make unnecessary all
the searches for information in which the reference librarian experiences what Miss Mudge used to refer to as 'the
joy of the chase' I think many of us would take a rather
dim view of it. However, I believe that patrons will continue to ask questions whose answers no one, not even an
experienced reference librarian, would ever think of feed-
ing into a machine and it may be a long, long time before
we can afford to buy the monsters anyway. (P. 282)

Rose Phelps was right; computerization without personalization would not be embraced by librarians. The care of AskA
services and others who participate in digital library development to provide quality, personal aid suggests that core librarian values remain intact. But other questions arise that are not
always fully addressed in our literature, and this paper concludes with concerns of anti-intellectualism coupled with com-
mercialism and the demise of libraries, social stratification and
deprofessionalization.

Anti-intellectualism and Hucksterism

In some ways, North American librarianship with its roots in
nineteenth century reverence for efficiency and scientific methods, can be said to be anti-intellectual. The idea that knowledge
can be organized and distilled into quickly retrievable units is
the hallmark of our success but is paradoxically our foil. With
each invention we reduce the size of our information (microfilm, CD-ROM, computer files, e-texts) and increase the sophistication of subject retrieval, selling this to users as being faster
and more powerful than previous methods. However, we ne-
glect that it is the time spent with the materials in reflection and
applying intelligence and imagination that creates the knowledge. We have not sped up information retrieval and increased
access so users can spend more time reading and reflecting in
quiet concentration; or if we have, we seem to forget to communicate that to our users. The VRD's goal is to network ex-

pertise in order to facilitate and enhance learning, providing "an amazing opportunity for first hand knowledge" (Lankes, 1998). There is always the concern of how to get information quickly and easily with an unsaid expectation that the knowledge will be absorbed more efficiently, too.

The promotional promise of a new and improved education is reminiscent of other educational products and curricula pushed on generations of public school teachers and anxious parents. Drawing instruction in the nineteenth century was viewed as necessary for survival and success in the job market, which resulted in the case of Massachusetts passing into law a means of free art instruction for men, women, and children (the Massachusetts Drawing Act, 1870) (Korzenik, 1985). The development of book clubs, reading groups, reviewing mechanisms, literary radio programs, and courses in the "Great Books" from the 1920s through 1950s is another example of selling access to information and knowledge by creating anxiety and a sense of inadequacy to the middle class (Rubin, 1992). This is not to say that these activities were not worthwhile and that digital libraries should not be developed; but the language of urgency and competition that feeds on inadequacy and anxiety should be analyzed for false promises, especially if those false promises are siphoning resources from existing educational institutions and weakening their ability to deliver services.

DEPROFESSIONALIZATION

Two activities of the VRD and the purpose of vrds in particular call into question the value of our work as librarians and K–12 teachers. First, the VRD and other vrds (Internet Public Library is an example) work on volunteer labor (Lankes, 1998; Internet Public Library, 1997). This is likely a temporary situation which suits an experimental prototype service. But in a period of tax revolts, calls for small government, and a general questioning on the value of publicly supported institutions, does the use of volunteers suggest that full-time paid experts will not be needed for answering reference questions? Second, the VRD, in connecting children to scientists, on the one hand is exciting and certainly admirable in that scientists are willing to volunteer time to children. On the other hand, what does this suggest about K–12 teacher authority to teach and answer questions? Is it necessary for a fourth grader to have access to a physicist? And will all children have this access to scientists or is it only for the gifted and talented?

Social Stratification

Frequently, the discussion of the have and have nots appears in the library and information science literature, and it is often at an unsophisticated level of discussion that concerns access to hardware and software. Certainly access to computers and technical support is part of the social stratification debate, and reports indicate that there is still an enormous gap in computer access for African American, Hispanic, and Native American populations (NTIA, 1999). But there is also the social stratification that comes about from education reproduction theory which posits that, through curriculum, schools re-create social stratification. Although emphasizing labor and the selection and certification of a workforce, reproduction theory has extended its definition to how schools preserve privilege by teaching "norms, values, dispositions, and culture that contribute to the ideological hegemony of dominant groups" (Apple, 1995). Coming under recent criticism for being insular, limited by small ethnographic studies, and weak on validity although strong analytically, reproduction theory provides a powerful construct for understanding curriculum difference (Davies, 1995; Ladwig, 1996; Kohn, 1998; Rochester, 1998). The curricular difference generally asserts itself as for the oppressed or denied class as: mechanical routine, rote learning, drills, right answers, rigidity, fragmented facts, and ways of behavior for submission, and for the privileged classes: creativity, abstraction, flexibility, independent thought, and liberation. Whose children will have the opportunity to experience a curriculum that values interaction with experts? Schooling may be for all, but education occurs for an elite. There is no evidence presented in the VRD to suggest that social stratification issues and curriculum tracking have been addressed in its research and development, which leaves the question of values open.

Service values for the digital age remain unformed and it can only be hoped that librarianship will embrace a values system that is inclusive, fair, and just for all users.

REFERENCES

ALA (American Library Association). Reference and Adult Services Division. Ad Hoc Committee on Behavioral Guidelines for Reference and Information Services. 1996. *Guidelines for Behavioral Performance of Reference and Information Services Professionals.* Available: *http://ala8.org.rusa/ stnd_behavior.html*

Apple, Michael W. 1995. *Education and Power.* 2d ed. New York: Routledge.

Bopp, Richard E. and Linda C. Smith. 1995. *Reference and Information Services: An Introduction.* 2d ed. Englewood, Colo.: Libraries Unlimited.

Davies, S. 1995. "Leaps of Faith: Shifting Currents in Critical Sociology of Education." *American Journal of Sociology* 100, no. 6 (May): 1448–78.

Ferguson, Chris D. and Charles A. Bunge. 1997. "The Shape of Services to Come: Values-Based Reference Service for the Largely Digital Library." *College & Research Libraries* 58 (May): 252–65.

Green, Samuel S. 1876. "Personal Relations Between Librarians and Readers." *Library Journal* 1 (October): 74.

"Internet Public Library: Same Metaphors, New Service." 1997. *American Libraries* 28, no. 2 (February): 56–59.

Jennerich, Elaine Z. and Edward J. Jennerich. 1997. *The Reference Interview as a Creative Art.* 2d ed. Englewood, Colo.: Libraries Unlimited.

Kessler, Andrew J. 1996. "Software that Pays for Itself." *Forbes* 158, no. 10 (October 21): 294.

Kohn, Alfie. 1998. "Only for My Kid: How Privileged Parents Undermine School Reform." *Phi Delta Kappan* 79, no. 8 (April): 568–78.

Korzenik, Diana. 1985. *Drawn to Art: A Nineteenth-Century American Dream.* Hanover, N.H.: University Press of New England.

Ladwig, James G. 1996. *Academic Distinctions: Theory and Methodology in the Sociology of School Knowledge.* New York: Routledge.

Lankes, R. David. 1998. *The Virtual Reference Desk: Building a Network of Expertise for America's Schools.* ERIC Clearinghouse on Information and Technology.

Lankes, R. David and Abby S. Kasowitz. 1998. *AskA Starter Kit: How to Build and Maintain Digital Reference Services.* Syracuse, N.Y.: ERIC Clearinghouse on Information & Technology.

Lubove, Seth. 1997. "Ron Katz, Enforcer." *Forbes* 160, no. 4 (August 25): 78.

Mangelsdorf, Martha E. 1995. "When Voice Mail Answers the Phones." *Inc.* 17, no. 8 (June): 96.

Michals, Debra. 1997. "Humans vs. Machines." *Working Woman* 22, no. 6 (June): 16–18.

NTIA (National Telecommunications and Information Administration). 1999.

Falling through the Net: Defining the Digital Divide. Falling through the Net Series on the Telecommunications and Information Technology Gap in America, no. 3. Available: *www.ntia.doc.gov/ntiahome/digitaldivide/*

Phelps, Rose B. 1957. "Reference Services in Public Libraries: The Last Quarter Century." *Wilson Library Bulletin* 32, no. 4 (December): 283–84.

Rochester, J. Martin. 1998. "What's It All About, Alfie? A Parent/Educator's Response to Alfie Kohn." *Phi Delta Kappan*, 80, no. 2 (October): 165–70.

Rothstein, Samuel. 1954. The Development of Reference Services in American Research Libraries. Ph.D. diss., University of Illinois.

Rubin, Joan Shelley. 1992. *The Making of Middle Brow Culture*. Chapel Hill, N.C.: University of North Carolina Press.

Sloan, Bernie. 1997. Service Perspectives for the Digital Library: Remote Reference Services. Available: *www.lis.uiuc.edu/~b-sloan/e-ref.html*

Tyckoson, David A. 1999. "What's Right with Reference." *American Libraries* 30, no. 5 (May): 57–63.

Weissman, Sara. 1998. Electronic Reference: Service Issues and Necessary Skills. In *AskA Starter Kit: How to Build and Maintain Digital Reference Services*, edited by R. David Lankes and Abby S. Kasowitz. Syracuse, N.Y.: ERIC Clearinghouse on Information & Technology.

Evolution or Entropy? The Changing Reference Culture and the Future of Reference Librarians*

Myoung C. Wilson

This paper addresses issues that relate to the changing functional relationship between the reference librarian and the user, based on the observation that the advance of information technology, particularly the Internet, has altered the values, attitudes, and beliefs of library users, and, as a consequence, their micro-culture. Highlights include: the traditional reference desk; the changed reference environment, including decreasing reference statistics in academic libraries, the creation of electronic reference services, and direct connections to information resources; user cultures; the convenience quotient (a measure of what type of user orientation is most comfortable within a given type of relationship and who regards the services provided as convenient); and components of reference service with regard to information resources.

INTRODUCTION

Where have you gone, Lloyds of London? In a recent article in *The Economist*, it was stated that the famous and venerable firm

---

* The author wishes to acknowledge the helpful comments she received from Professor Richard W. Wilson, author of *Compliance Ideologies: Rethinking Political Culture* (Cambridge University Press, 1992) and a member of the Department of Political Science at Rutgers University.

of Lloyds faces a fundamental, perhaps insoluble, problem. This comes from "electronic rivals doing what they do but faster and more cheaply; Lloyds has to explain why what it does is worth doing at all" (Clubhouse, 1999). The same question might be asked of reference librarians; why is it that what we do is worth doing?

Culture is defined as socially transmitted values, attitudes and beliefs. *Micro-culture* refers to a particular relationship pattern, while *macro-culture* is the overall configuration of various micro patterns (Wilson, 2000: 253). I submit that the advance of information technology, particularly the Internet, has altered the values, attitudes and beliefs of contemporary library users and, as a consequence, the micro-culture of library users. These changes affect user valuations of reference services and call for a revised service model that will offer optimum services appropriate for the information age.

This paper addresses issues that relate to the changing functional relationship between the reference librarian and the user. In order for any service to be provided effectively, it must relate to the needs and expectations of those who use it. There must be a reciprocal relationship between the values and attitudes of those who provide services and the values and attitudes of those who use the service. Without this, the relationship will cease to be reciprocally interactive. Calls for the reinvigoration of the role of reference librarians or assertions that reference librarians must be the keystone of future libraries, and/or of the information environment (Nardi and O'Day, 1999: 80), thus miss the point. The only way that reference librarians can define their future role is to identify the ways that the reciprocal relationship between reference librarians and users is evolving.

THE TRADITIONAL REFERENCE DESK

In the past two years, conferences such as the Virtual Reference Desk Digital Reference Conference have been organized to allow reference librarians to search collectively for an appropriate future role.[1] Virtually all of the papers resulting from such conferences reiterate that traditional reference services are here to stay, modified only by the use of improved tools. I argue instead that something has been altered decisively in the user culture and that we must comprehend this changed culture and fundamentally transform our role to accord with it.

The traditional reference desk (and reference service) existed in an environment where information resources were highly concentrated and where the reference librarian was knowledgeable about the content, location, and accessibility of these resources. The relationship between the librarian and the user was a hierarchical one with the reference librarian functioning as a gatekeeper to these resources. In these traditional libraries, users and reference librarians formed an important and stable micro-cultural relationship via the reference desk. In the process of gaining information or providing access to information resources, reference services had a clearly defined, major role in information provision. Individual users at their desktops had virtually no choices regarding metadata, information resources, and information access. In these libraries, the reference desk was one of the few places where users could obtain help. Interaction patterns were highly structured and predictable. The key to this relationship was that it favored those users who were most comfortable in a hierarchical context in which reference librarians possessed expertise regarding information resources and access. Independent and individualistic users, underrepresented in the literature, often chafed over the constraints that this kind of relationship imposed. Reference librarians in traditional libraries are familiar with users who are uncomfortable asking questions and participating in the reference service process.

THE CHANGED REFERENCE ENVIRONMENT

It has been reported that reference desk statistics are generally decreasing in American academic libraries (Palmer, 1999: 143). At my own library at Rutgers, reference statistics declined 21 percent during the academic year 1997–98 (equivalent to one out of five individual requests) and 24 percent during the academic year 1998–99. Many other institutions report a comparable decline in the numbers of those seeking assistance.

At the same time that there has been a decline in reference desk statistics, many libraries have created electronic reference services, most frequently referred to as "Ask A Librarian." At Rutgers, the Ask A Librarian service logged almost 2,500 queries during the academic year 1998–99.[2] The quantitative measurement of reference services as such, therefore, should not be confined to the reference desk alone. Many reference questions now arrive via individual reference librarians' e-mail accounts, either from students seeking further assistance for classroom work or from faculty members who are on research leave or are working in their offices. At my own institution, we have quantified these requests through a new statistical form that reflects reference activities away from the reference desk.

Consider for a moment the past when users would come to the reference desk with simple requests, such as for a map of a country or for zip code information. Many of the traditional print-based ready reference sources such as the U.S. Zip Code Directory and country maps are now available on the Internet as part of a growing number of e-reference tools (i.e., an electronic ready reference collection that libraries are organizing as part of their Websites). The electronic ready reference tools that are accessible from the user's desktop contain answers to ready reference queries, thus bypassing the reference desk where such information was traditionally provided. In the past, interlibrary loan requests at my library at Rutgers were verified at the reference desk. Now, users can place an online request via a Web page. Also, Rutgers users can renew their own books and can get reference or, as mentioned earlier, other assistance via "Ask a Librarian" services from wherever they are. Thus, information and services that were once provided at the reference desk are transferred to a Website. In other words, many of the keys formerly held in the hands of reference librarians that were the basis for their gatekeeper function have now been transferred to library Web pages and are beyond the direct control of reference librarians.

Is it any wonder then that librarians are noticing a decline in reference desk activities? Clearly, given the decrease, it should be no cause for dismay when people ask if it is time to downsize the reference desk. The more meaningful question is how do we "right-size" the reference desk, both literally and figuratively? To *right-size* the reference desk means both physical changes in the traditional reference desk as well as a revision of the service content. For example, is the physical size of the traditional reference desk too large in proportion to the decline that has taken place in reference activities? Are computers at the reference desk placed in such a way that users can easily follow the librarians' navigational paths? E-mail reference services, Web-based subject guides, in-person research counseling sessions, and other services that are not bound to a physical reference desk can be integrated into a reconfigured reference service. Other possibilities such as reference services at student centers or shopping malls should be continuously explored.

In the post-Internet age of decentralized and distributed information resources, reference librarians no longer have a franchise as sole providers of information at the reference desk (Benton Foundation, 1996: 13). Consequently, the importance of the reference desk as a central node of information provision has been questioned in recent years. Users have begun to make direct connections to information sources via the new media-networked databases or e-mail, chatrooms, newsgroups, etc.

USER CULTURES

Culture theory holds that individuals in all societies choose one of five different ways of life for themselves. This approach has received a great deal of acclaim as well as vigorous criticism. It is beyond the scope of this paper to elaborate the theory in detail. Suffice it to say that individuals choose ways of life that have been variously termed fatalistic, hierarchical, individualistic, egalitarian, and communitarian. The importance of these ways of life, or subcultures, in any society is ascertained by research into the relative prevalence of these behavior patterns (Wilson, 2000: 252). I contend that the way users interact with the reference desk can be better understood by linking patterns of user behavior with the categories identified by culture theory. Making these connections, it is possible to characterize the ways that users seek and use information resources. In the relationship between the reference librarian and the user, it thus becomes crucially important to ascertain what types of user orientations are most congruent with the relationship context. Only then can reference librarians begin to design appropriate service models and define their new role.

CONVENIENCE QUOTIENTS

Ann Lipow (1999) argues that convenience is what governs the choice of where to go for assistance. To elaborate this argument, the relationship between the user and the reference librarian can be viewed in terms of a concept that can be called a "convenience quotient." In other words, which types of people (according to culture theory) are most comfortable within a given type of librarian-user relationship, and which types of people regard the reference services provided as convenient? I suggest that in the traditional reference service structure, individuals with hierarchical orientations were most comfortable while others, especially those with individualistic and egalitarian orientations (i.e. those who enjoy working on their own and those who desire greater equality in the way that users and reference librarians interact), were less comfortable. In other words, the culture of reference services overall favored a pattern in which those whose orientations were hierarchical were best served, with the user in the role of supplicant and the reference librarian in the role of gatekeeper. This does not mean, of course, that reference services were unavailable to others. It does mean that those who were not hierarchical in orientation were less comfortable in the reference situation (i.e. they had a low convenience quotient). Hence, for them, the nature of the provision of reference services could often be decidedly inconvenient.

With the advent of the Internet, the nature of information provision has been radically reversed, thus appealing to the opposite type of user from those accommodated in a traditional reference service environment. The type of users best served in this new context are those who are individualistic or egalitarian. In this context it is the hierarchical individual as supplicant who is now on the periphery while individualistic and egalitarian users have taken center stage. Concomitantly, there has been a drastic decline in the gatekeeper function of reference librarians.

In this new context it is the autonomous user of Internet resources who finds the new reference relationship pattern most congenial. In fact, the undue intrusion of reference librarians into this new reference context may be felt by many such users to be both inappropriate and inconvenient; previously, individualistic and egalitarian users were uncomfortable intruding on the time of reference librarians. At the same time, users who attempt to reassert a hierarchical relationship where the librarian is gatekeeper may be perceived by reference librarians as lacking computer literacy skills.

Regardless of the type of user, reference librarians must enhance their role as technological gatekeeper, guiding users through an overload of information sources. In order to perform this role, reference librarians must not only improve their technological skills, but they must also learn about the new types of users who have taken center stage. Koyama (1998) suggests that cyberspace users "prefer anonymity to in-person, over-the-desk delivery of reference service and feel free of the captive nature inherent sometimes in the personal interview controlled by the librarian" (p. 51). These are the very type of unreachable users who might have shied away from the traditional reference desk. Reference librarians now have an opportunity to interact with them via cyberspace. The context, however, is radically different from the one reference librarians knew in the past.

REASSESSING REFERENCE SERVICE

The context of reference service has changed. If functional reciprocity is to be reclaimed between the user and the reference librarian, it can only occur if reference librarians understand and accept the changes in their role that have taken place. The advent of the Internet has decisively altered the culture of library users and the relative importance of new user types, such as electronic browsers (Wilson, 1999). Bemoaning the loss of the traditional relationship pattern is no substitute for reassessing what the new role of reference librarians must be; no effort to reassert a traditional reference librarian role in the digital environment can possibly succeed in the context of the new reference service.

The first step is to recognize that reference service with regard to information resources has three components. The first component is service that provides users with information about information (metadata) as well as factual information from the ready reference sources. This service is being rapidly bifurcated (and is thus a source of confusion for users) between reference services and the products of companies like Yahoo!. It is also the area that is being aggressively explored by e-commerce enterprises and software vendors. Modeling themselves after the well-publicized electronic auction company eBay, a new commercial venture called InfoRocket will launch a Website allowing anyone to buy and sell answers to questions over the Internet (Maney, 1999). One can imagine all of the issues of reliability, accuracy, and copyright that may be associated with this venture. Nevertheless, the commercial provision of much of this traditional type of ready reference service will continue to be explored by for-profit entrepreneurs.

The second component in measuring reference service is training users to access and evaluate information sources. The ability to access and evaluate the validity of information sources is a key element in developing information literacy. The role of reference librarians in training users has been on the rise, either in person, in classroom situations or, increasingly, via cyberspace. In fact, this function has become so important that a good argument can be made for the provision of teaching positions at all libraries, especially academic ones.

The third component in measuring reference service is what lately has been called the "invisible function" of reference librarians. This aspect of service is grounded in the fact that many users are not clearly aware of their initial information needs. Nardi and O'Day use the expression "information therapy" to describe the time-honored reference interview process (1999: 85-92). While components two and three have always existed, it is now clear that they are increasingly becoming the most important aspects of service provided by reference librarians.

CONCLUSION

It is not the case, as some aver, that reference librarians will become an extinct or endangered species. The advent of new technology has changed the behavior of users in a way that requires a reciprocal change in the behavior of reference librarians toward greater emphasis on the previously described components two and three. Librarians in the future will need to be flexible, adaptable, and conversant with how the new individualistic and egalitarian user seeks information. Unfortunately, little study or research has been done to understand how this category of user seeks and uses information in the electronic environment. Ironically, the very technology employed by individualistic users can enable librarians to gather data about them (i.e., the ways that they use library resources and services). The rapidly emerging e-commerce ventures are famous (or infamous) for collecting data on their customers for future product development and marketing. If Amazon.com's "push" technology can identify titles of potential interest to its customers, then the technology used by the libraries can help librarians to identify what kinds of services, databases, subject categories, and so on, are in demand.

Only by identifying and forging a new relationship between users and reference librarians, both at the reference desk and beyond, can reference culture be recalibrated. The emergence of a digital and distributed information environment has temporarily unhinged a relationship that has been stable for the past one hundred years. The continuing viability of reference librarians now depends on how reference librarians and users mutually adapt as librarians take on more of a role in assisting users in accessing information and clarifying their information needs. Until then reference librarians around the world will continue to be adrift over the relatively sudden and massive alterations that have occurred in the reference culture.

> Changes in micro-culture occur when there are "shifts by individuals away from allegiance to one pattern . . . as a consequence of a cumulative mismatch between the promise and the performance of a particular relationship pattern. (Wilson, 2000: 253)

If we are to maintain user allegiance to the value of reference service, we need to align with the new reference/user cultural reality. Some reference librarians are beginning to fine-tune their virtual reference interview skills (Viles, 1999) in order to add a human element to the new machine dominated environment. They have begun as well to develop new ways to reach out to once unreachable users by creating and developing new electronic reference services. The papers in this book are evidence of these endeavors. All these activities point to an exciting future for reference librarians who are just beginning to forge links with the next generation of users. These emerging new micro-cultural aspects of relationship patterns between the user and the reference librarian will define the attributes of the macro-cultural structure of future reference services.

NOTES

1. One such conference was Finding Common Ground: Creating the Library of the Future Without Diminishing the Library of the Past organized by the Harvard Library and the other was the Library of Congress Institute: Reference Service in A Digital Age, both held in 1998. Many similar themes have been the focus of other conferences.
2. For a more detailed analysis of these queries, see the Annual Report, "Ask A Librarian," compiled by Natalie Borisovets, Rutgers Ask a Librarian Coordinator, available at: *newark.rutgers.edu/~natalieb/ask9899.htm*

REFERENCES

Benton Foundation. 1996. *Buildings, Books and Bytes: Libraries and Communities in the Digital Age: A Report on the Public's Opinion of Library Leaders' Visions for the Future.* Washington, D.C.: Benton Foundation. Available: *www.benton.org/Library/Kellog/home.html*

"Clubhouse for Sale." 1999. *The Economist* (14 August): 59.

Koyama, Janice T. 1998. *"http://digiref.scenarios.*issues" *Reference and User Services Quarterly* 38 no. 1: 51.

Lipow, Anne G. 1999. Serving the Remote User: Reference Service in the Digital Environment. Paper presented at Information Online & On Disk, 20 January, Sydney, Australia. Available: *http://www.csu.edu.au/special/online99/proceedings99/200.htm*

Maney, Kevin. 1999. Site to Auction Information. *USA Today,* 9 September. Available: *www.usatoday.com/life/cyber/tech/ctg076.htm*

Nardi, Bonnie A. and Vicki L. O'Day. 1999. *Information Ecologies: Using Technology with Heart*. Cambridge, Mass.: MIT Press.

Palmer, Susan Szasz. 1999. Creating Our Role as Reference Librarians of the Future: Fate or Choice? In *Racing Toward Tomorrow: Proceedings of the ACRL Ninth National Conference*. Chicago: Association of College and Research Libraries.

Viles, Ann. 1999. The Virtual Reference Interview: Equivalencies: A Discussion Proposal. Paper distributed at the International Federation of Library Associations and Institutions (IFLA) Discussion Group on Reference Work, Bangkok.

Wilson, Myoung C. 1999. "The Leopard that Changed Its Spots: Official Publications as a Research Tool in an Evolving Information Environment." *INSPEL* 33, no. 2: 113.

Wilson, Richard W. 2000. "The Many Voices of Political Culture: Assessing Different Approaches." *World Politics* 52 (January, 2000): 253.

Part II

Building Digital Reference Services and Networks

OVERVIEW

Digital reference offers new opportunities for collaboration among libraries and information services. This type of collaboration goes beyond interlibrary loan and resource sharing between a few institutions. Networks of digital reference services allow the matching of patron queries to the most appropriate expert, whether a reference librarian in a particular region or a subject expert in a particular field, and the development of cross-service archives of questions and answers. Kresh and Arret describe the process of developing such a network, the Library of Congress' Collaborative Digital Reference Service.

Building networks of digital reference services requires the definition of consistent processes and standards. Bennett, Kasowitz, and Lankes highlight the standards-setting process for digital reference services in the Virtual Reference Desk network. These standards of service management and provision can be applied to individual digital reference services as well as those participating in collaborative networks.

Collaborative Digital Reference Service: Update on LC Initiative

Diane Kresh and Linda Arret

This paper provides a status report on the Library of Congress' efforts to create a digital reference service in order to provide reliable and credible reference service by subject experts and experienced librarians. This service will serve users anytime, anywhere, through an international collaborative network of participating national, academic, public, and special libraries. This paper describes background leading to the development of the Collaborative Digital Reference Service (CDRS), including trends in digital library work, meetings organized by the Library of Congress, and statistics illustrating the growing numbers of researchers using the Internet. Plans for building and testing the CDRS are also discussed.

BACKGROUND

The Collaborative Digital Reference Service (CDRS) described here began in the Library of Congress (LC) as a conversation and a vision. Current plans are to have a production service in place to provide professional reference service to users anywhere anytime, through an international, digital network of libraries.

In 1997, we concluded that for all the excellent work underway on digital libraries, the focus had been on collecting, cataloging, and preserving digital collections; there had been little coordinated or collaborative focus on library services addressing other digital issues. Two public service concerns that were getting deserved attention then related to providing public Internet access in libraries and providing services to remote users of libraries. In each case, the reference librarian was at the center of the concern. Emphasis was on determining how best to connect the reference librarian with the needs of the on-site and the remote library user, especially at a time when electronic resources were increasing at an astounding rate. It was clear that the nature of reference work itself, particularly its very collaborative aspect, could guide us in identifying some next steps.

EXPLORING DIGITAL REFERENCE ROLES AND POSSIBILITIES

After a collaborative brainstorming session and an open discussion at an ALA midwinter conference in January 1998, we decided to convene a conference called Reference Service in a Digital Age, the first of its kind to address the issues of digital reference directly. The goal was for reference librarians to come together to address their services and needs at a time when the death knell for libraries was being sounded. Pundits hastened to proclaim the demise of the book and printed reference sources, and many in the academic community were concerned about students consulting only the Web for their research.

The keynote speaker at the conference, Bonnie A. Nardi, shared thoughts on libraries as rich information ecologies and the crucial role of one of the keystone species, the reference librarian. Through a combination of mediation and quality control, the reference librarian maintains and enriches both the locality and the diversity of the vastly expanding universe of information resources. The librarian brings to the information seeker the power of local loyalties and the scope of global diversity (Nardi, 1998). The question remained: how do we maintain and enrich our connections to our users to bring them this power and diversity? Many evaluations at the conference told us that increased cooperation among libraries, regionally and nationally, with continued leadership by the Library of Congress, was essential to the future of high-quality reference service that integrated both electronic and print resources.

An open session was convened at the ALA 1999 Midwinter Meeting in Philadelphia[1], and a meeting was held in Washington D.C. to discuss options with a variety of librarians. A Collaborative Digital Reference Service was conceived. It would start small and grow into a vast international service that would allow libraries to help each other serve all their users, no matter where the users are. From the beginning, interest was expressed by all types of libraries around the world.

NEED FOR A COLLABORATIVE DIGITAL REFERENCE SERVICE

Researchers are everywhere. In the United States alone, 57 million adults use the Internet from home; this represents an increase of 50 percent over the last year. The number of U.S. households using the Internet is over 46 million, up from 14.9 million in 1995 (The Strategis Group, 2000). Worldwide, Internet use is expected to grow 25 percent annually (McGarvey, 2000). By 2003, non-English material may account for over half the content on the Internet (Nua Ltd. and others, 2000a); Latin America is experiencing over 42 percent growth in Internet use annually (Nua Ltd. and others, 2000b); wireless access is expected to increase over 700 percent by 2003 (Nua Ltd. and others, 2000c). At the beginning of the year 2000, there were over one billion pages on the Internet (Inktomi, 2000). In 1999, no single search engine covered more than 16 percent of the Internet (Lawrence and Giles, 1999), and together, the top 10 search engines covered barely 50 percent of the Internet. The communications options increased in numbers and variety; people could do research and ask questions in person, in writing, by phone and fax, and online at least by e-mail, chatrooms, and video conferencing.

Librarians are aware that the Internet is not the same as a library. The Internet is:

- located everywhere and anywhere;
- disorganized, unstructured, and flat;
- unverifiable;
- digital only; and
- doubling in growth each year.

In addition, some commercial Internet search services offer non-expert volunteers for help; search engines do not cover very much content; and there are no controlled vocabularies or other library tools to relate like items.

On the other hand, libraries:

- are physical locations, although people also use them remotely;
- are organized and structured;
- maintain collections that are evaluated via collection guidelines;
- experience continued growth;
- are comprehensive (both analogue and digital works);
- employ skilled, trained subject and language and navigation experts;
- provide analogue and digital catalogs, indexes, and bibliographies; and
- offer controlled vocabularies and other collocating and standards tools.

PLANNING FOR CDRS

By linking libraries, the CDRS will combine the power of local collections and staff strengths with the diversity and availability of libraries and librarians everywhere, 24 hours a day, 7 days a week. A librarian will be available at all times to offer users trained help in the access to collections and resources, both analogue and digital. For example, academic libraries in the United States have over 750 million books, serials, and government documents, over 420 million of which are available only in a particular library (R. R. Bowker, 1998: 426); and we note that these works are whole works, not just pages. These statistics do not include public, special, and school libraries in the United States, nor any libraries outside the United States. Most items in libraries are not digitized and will never be digitized. At this time, the numerous Web-based answer services search neither these vast nondigitized collections nor the thousands of library online catalogs that describe and manage and collocate the collections.

CDRS can provide the services necessary to help researchers to be productive and use information around the clock from any location. In particular it will meet the following requirements:

- information will be organized and available in order to have intellectual and economic value;
- information will be constantly refreshed with new material; and
- the hands-on touch of the skilled reference librarian will provide context and added value.

During the course of three planned pilot phases, we are examining three components of the CDRS—set-up component, question and answer component, and post Q&A component—as well as the administrative threads that run through all three. We are incrementally testing the exchange of questions and answers among libraries in the pilot. Profiles of each library enable us to deliver an incoming question to the most appropriate and available library worldwide. Through a request manager function, to be embedded later in a software product, we hope to be able to receive, examine, store, distribute, log, and track questions, and to deliver credible and contextual answers that can be stored in an archive that becomes a resource on the network.

The CDRS will supplement the services that libraries offer. Libraries and their local users will be the main beneficiaries of a service that works globally while enabling locally. Users will work through their libraries; questions that cannot be answered locally can be contributed to the service by CDRS member libraries. Membership service level agreements will define the nature of a local library's relationship to the CDRS and will be codified in library profiles. These profiles will be searched by a request manager to determine the best place to send a question to meet the subject and deadline needs of the user.

The first pilot ended in March 2000. The libraries that participated in the pilot include: Library of Congress, National Agricultural Library, National Library of Australia, National Library of Canada, Smithsonian American Art Museum, University of Texas at Austin, Cornell University, Santa Monica Public Library, Morris County (N.J.) Public Library, and the Peninsula Library System of the Bay Area in northern California. All participants contributed edited sample questions and answers to be sent on a scripted schedule. The primary learning objectives for the pilot were to test the data and standards and searching in the library profile database, and the use of e-mail vs. a Web form for submitting questions.

In the second pilot, we expect to raise the bar by including more institutions worldwide, increasing the volume of questions, revising the profile database, experimenting with software packages to serve as request manager, storing questions for eventual loading into an archive, reviewing the data format for this archive, developing a variety of service level agreements, identifying staff training needs, and identifying the roles of a CDRS collaborative governing board. The third pilot will likely focus on scaling up the workflow, determining the needs for back-up systems, and developing a true question and answer archive that becomes a network resource in its own right.

CONCLUSION

The CDRS will deliver the direct benefits of quality reference service to a broad spectrum of users anytime anywhere—a reliable and authoritative knowledge navigation service, a large searchable archive of authoritative answers, and increased visibility and support for libraries everywhere. The service will deliver the indirect benefits of quality support for education and research; the promotion of productivity, commerce, and scientific endeavor; and the basic coin of democracy: value-added information.

For the Library of Congress, the CDRS helps fulfill one of its missions: to provide quality reference services through its international collections of broad subject, language, and format scope, as well as the traditional cataloging systems that support electronic reference. It continues a long LC tradition of collaboration with other libraries and a tradition of leadership in information services. But the Library of Congress does not and cannot do this alone. By enabling locally with libraries everywhere, LC and its partners bring control and context to the global and diverse world of information.

NOTES

1. The meeting summary from the January 31, 1999 open session is available at: *http://lcweb.loc.gov/rr/digiref/phil99.html*

REFERENCES

Inktomi. 2000. "Web Surpasses One Billion Documents." Press Release. [Online]. Available: *www.inktomi.com/new/press/billion.html* [24 April 2000].

Lawrence, Steve and C. Lee Giles. 1999. "Accessibility of Information on the Web." *Nature* 400, no. 6740 (8 July): 107.

McGarvey, Joe. 2000. "Deflating Bandwidth Glut Predictions." *Inter@ctive Week* (February 21, 2000). [Online]. Available: *www.zdnet.com/intweek/stories/news/0%2C4164%2C2441081%2C00.html* [24 April 2000].

Nardi, Bonnie A. 1998. "Information Ecologies." Keynote Address at the Library of Congress Institute: Reference Service in a Digital Age, Washington, D.C., June 1998. Available: *lcweb.loc.gov/rr/digiref/nardi.html*

Nua Ltd. and others, 2000a. "Internationalisation of the Web." (Mar 29, 1999). [Online]. Available: *www.nua.ie/surveys/?f=VS&art_id=905354800&rel=true* [26 April 2000].

Nua Ltd. and others, 2000b. "Latin American Market Continues to Boom." (Feb 1, 2000). [Online]. Available: *www.nua.ie/surveys?f=VS&art_id=905355563&rel=true* [26 April 2000].

Nua Ltd. and others, 2000c. "Wireless Internet To Surpass PC Internet." (Feb 10, 2000). [Online]. Available: *www.nua.ie/surveys/?f=VS&art_id=905355585&rel=true* [26 April 2000].

R. R. Bowker. 1998. *The Bowker Annual of Library and Book Trade Information.* 43rd ed. New York: R.R. Bowker.

The Strategis Group, 2000. "More than Half of all U.S. Adults Now Online." [Online]. *www.strategisgroup.com/press/pubs/IUTFinal.htm* [24 April 2000].

Digital Reference Quality Criteria

Blythe Allison Bennett, Abby Kasowitz, and R. David Lankes

This paper identifies and describes a set of quality criteria for AskA, or digital reference, services. These services are Internet-based, human-mediated information services and are operated by libraries, individual subject experts, and organizations providing subject expertise. The criteria presented in this paper are designed for the Virtual Reference Desk (VRD) Network, a group representing subject-area and library digital reference services geared in part to the education community; however, the criteria can serve as a model for digital reference services in general. This paper presents the criteria in the context of digital reference evaluation, describes the process by which the criteria were created and revised, and describes the criteria as they apply to the VRD Network members.

INTRODUCTION

While there has been research defining quality criteria for in-person reference, there has been little in the field of digital reference (Kasowitz, Bennett, and Lankes, 2000). This paper identifies and describes a set of standards by which to assess individual digital reference services. For the purpose of this paper, the term "digital reference service" is used to represent all Internet-based, human-mediated information services, including those based in library settings and other types of organizations. Digital reference services are also referred to as AskA services, as in "AskA Scientist" and "Ask An Art Expert." Service

staff members responsible for answering user queries are referred to as experts, whether their expertise is in a specific subject area or a process, such as information referral. This paper
addresses digital reference services in a variety of contexts that
serve different groups of users including the education community (e.g., students, parents, and educators).

QUALITY CRITERIA IN REFERENCE SERVICE

Digital reference can borrow some criteria established for identifying quality characteristics of traditional reference service.
Both forms of reference share the goal of helping users meet information needs. Many of the same processes and characteristics are considered important, including easily accessible service,
instruction to users on finding information independently,
knowledgeable staff, and interactivity to confirm the user's
need. However, the nature of the digital reference environment
requires new applications and interpretations of quality characteristics. For instance, interactivity in traditional reference con-
sists of an effective face-to-face reference interview, while
interactivity in digital reference can include exchange of e-mail
messages or capturing of important information through a Web-
based query form.

Identifying Digital Reference Service Criteria

In 1997, Lankes (1998) convened an expert panel of representa-
tives from subject-specific and information referral digital reference services to identify quality criteria of K–12-related AskA
services and to select existing AskA services that fit the criteria. Original panel members included Blythe Bennett of
KidsConnect, Lynn Bry of the MAD Scientist Network, Martha
Dexter of the Library of Congress, Peter Milbury of LM_NET,
Joan Stahl of the National Museum of American Art/
Smithsonian, Robin Summers of AskERIC, Steve Weimar of the
Math Forum, and Ken Williams of the Math Forum. The work
of the panel was conducted via a listserv and other Internet
tools. The initial work of the panel (criteria and selection) was
completed by the end of August 1997. Throughout the year, the

panel was called upon to provide advice, opinions and input on digital reference quality criteria as well as general service issues.

This six month electronic discussion resulted in a list of 12 quality characteristics of digital reference service[1]:

1. Authoritative
2. Accessible
3. Fast (turnaround of response)
4. Private (protects user information)
5. Consistent with good reference practice
6. Clear in user expectations
7. Reviewed regularly
8. Provides access to related information
9. Noncommercial
10. Publicized
11. Instructive
12. Offers training to experts

This list, based upon panel members' experiences in managing and coordinating exemplary digital reference services for the K–12 education community and other audiences, was later adapted into the document, "Facets of Quality for K–12 Digital Reference Services" (Kasowitz et al., 1999).

This document was then revised by the VRD Expert Panel 99 (April to August 1999) to include input from Patricia Memmott (Internet Public Library) and Sara Weissman (Morris County Public Library, N.J.). There was a third discussion of the criteria at an October 13, 1999 meeting of expert panel members and other digital reference service representatives. The group in attendance included many veteran panel members as well as new participants from a variety of services.

REVISING STANDARDS FOR A REFERENCE SERVICE NETWORK

The Virtual Reference Desk (VRD)[2] coordinates a collaborative network of digital reference services called the VRD Network. This network is part of the AskA Consortium, a group of organizations dedicated to supporting AskA services and setting standards for service quality and network cooperation. The primary benefit of participation for AskA services is the ability to off-load out-of-scope and overflow questions (those that exceed the service's capacity for response) to the network for redistribution. Sixteen services participated in the pilot test of the collaborative network in the fall of 1999, including subject-specific and library services. The standards discussed in this paper will help define membership requirements for current and future participants, including newly created AskA services.

The revised standards, based on the "Facets of Quality," exist as a working document designed to maintain consistency in VRD's collaborative network of AskA services and provide quality digital reference service to the education community. While many of the AskA services are geared toward the K–12 community, some of the services welcome queries from adult patrons. The document will be revised as needed with input from network members. Participating services currently include:

- MAD Scientist Network (Washington University Medical School)
- Ask the Space Scientist (NASA)
- Ask Dr. Math (The Math Forum)
- Ask Dr. Universe (Washington State University)
- AskERIC (Educational Resources Information Center)
- Ask Jake the Sea Dog (WhaleTimes SeaBed)
- Ask Shamu (Sea World/Busch Gardens)
- Kentucky Center for School Safety (Eastern Kentucky University)
- Digital Library and Archives (Virginia Tech)
- Dino Russ's Lair (Illinois State Geological Survey)
- The ENC Virtual Reference Desk (Eisenhower National Clearinghouse)
- Ask EPA (Environmental Protection Agency)
- Internet Public Library (University of Michigan)
- American Memory (Library of Congress)
- Morris County Public Library (NJ)
- Ask Joan of Art (National Museum of American Art)
- Teacher2Teacher (Math Forum)
- Science Line (ScienceNet)

CRITERIA FOR VRD NETWORK MEMBERSHIP

Digital reference services differ from each other in many aspects including policy and procedure, scope, audience, expertise, and available resources. Services participating in the VRD Network must adhere to a basic level of quality for each of the criteria listed below. Each item in the criteria contains a range of levels of adherence; the goal of the collaboration is to assist each service in reaching a higher standard of service to its patrons. Some services already meet a high standard for many criteria, although each has the capability to increase service in some areas.

The criteria are divided into two main categories: user transaction and service development/management. The user transaction category includes those components that deal with the question-answering process such as accessibility, prompt turnaround, clear response policy, and the interactive and instructive nature of the service. The service development/management category involves decisions made in creating and maintaining the service that affect overall quality and user satisfaction: authoritative, trained experts, private, reviewed, provides access to related information, and publicized.

The following section presents each of the criteria, its definition, and examples of how it can be met. The quality criteria are presented in the context of AskA services that provide responses to the education community; however, they can be applied to digital reference services in all contexts and for all audiences.

User Transaction

1. **Accessible**—Digital reference services for the K–12 community should be reachable and navigable easily by any Internet user regardless of equipment sophistication, physical disability, or language barrier. The service should be reachable by either e-mail or by Web-based query forms. The Web presence should be in compliance with the Americans with Disabilities Act (ADA).[3] Some services may even wish to include access to English as well as non-English speakers.

2. **Prompt Turnaround**—Questions should be addressed as quickly as possible. Actual turnaround time depends on a service's question-answer policy and available resources (e.g., staffing, funds, etc.). Services should respond to at least 10 percent of incoming questions within two business days. They should acknowledge user questions within two to five days of receipt and notify users if they will not receive a response. The ultimate goal would be to respond to 100 percent of appropriate (in scope) incoming questions within one to two business days.

3. **Clear Response Policy**—Clear communication should occur either before or at the start of every digital reference transaction in order to reduce opportunities for user confusion and inappropriate inquiries. A service must create and adhere to a clear response policy.

Question-answering procedures and services should be stated clearly in an accessible place on the service's Website or in an acknowledgment message to the user. The statement should indicate question scope, types of answers provided, and expected turnaround time.

4. **Interactive**—Digital reference services should provide opportunities for an effective reference interview, so that users can communicate necessary information to experts and to clarify vague user questions. Services should encourage sharing of important user information such as grade level and question subject area either through a Web-based query form or follow-up e-mail message, without compromising user privacy. Services could incorporate a follow-up method, such as assigning tracking numbers to questions, in order to identify related messages. Real-time reference interviews could be made available to ensure a clarified question.

5. **Instructive**—Services should offer pointers and paths used to find the best resources, so users can learn to answer similar questions on their own. For example, responses can include the tools used to find resources (e.g., search engines, indexes, bibliographies, catalogs), specific search terms and processes used,

and series of steps taken. (Subject experts that draw upon their own backgrounds and knowledge of a particular topic should describe problem-solving processes and provide additional pointers when possible.)

When an answer or resources cannot be found, services should provide the user with a description of paths, keywords, and processes that were attempted. Library-based services should promote information literacy by responding with detailed search paths and sets of resources that either provide the answer or allow the user to investigate on his or her own. Subject experts will provide answers drawing upon their own backgrounds and knowledge of a particular topic, and will provide additional pointers when appropriate.

Service Development and Management

6. **Authoritative**—Experts of a digital reference service should have the necessary knowledge and educational background in the service's given subject area or skill, in order to qualify as an expert. Specific levels of knowledge, skill, and experience are determined by each service and its related discipline or field. There should be at least one qualified expert who can oversee the quality and accuracy of staff responses. The service should be staffed with professionals (paid or volunteer) in the subject specialty of the AskA service. In information referral services, staff should consist of professional librarians.

Users should be notified of the authority of the service in general as well as individual experts through an e-mailed acknowledgment or on a Website. Participating organizations can provide evidence of certification for professionals who answer questions. The service should communicate any possible perspectives that may be reflected in responses to questions. Library-based services provide a balance of viewpoints on a subject if applicable, but subject specific services sometimes provide a particular perspective on a subject. For example, a question about the creation of the earth would receive a response with a scientific perspective from a science AskA service, while a library-based service might provide a variety of perspectives found in different types of resources.

7. **Trained Experts**—Services should offer orientation or training processes to prepare experts (librarians or subject experts) to respond to inquiries using clear and effective language and following service response policies and procedures. Training of experts is one of the most important aspects of planning and operating a digital reference service. The service should develop, pilot test, and provide a training component that could include written documents containing response guidelines, opportunities for experts to practice responding to inquiries accompanied by feedback on performance, or mentoring by more experienced staff. The service should ensure that trainees achieve mastery of training objectives and that each trainee's performance during and after training be documented.

If the experts are volunteers, they should be recognized in some way for their successful completion of the process. One suggestion is to offer credit for successful completion of the training session, whether it is for continuing education, basic course work, or professional advancement (e.g., through the workplace, the certifying organization, etc.).

8. **Private**—All communications between users and experts should be held in complete privacy. There should be no public access to user names, e-mail or mailing addresses, or questions unless there is written notice prior to the information being made available, such as on a Web-based query form. Privacy policies should be posted on the Website, especially the page with the Web-based query form.[4] If question and answer pairs are to be posted in a public archive, all identifying information about the user should be removed. Special attention should be paid to services for children under 18, such as obtaining parental permission if identifying information is posted publicly.

9. **Reviewed**—Digital reference services should evaluate their processes and services regularly. Ongoing review and assessment helps ensure quality, efficiency, and reliability of transactions as well as overall user satisfaction. Services can monitor responses either before sending them to users or at some point afterwards on a periodic basis. Corrections and follow-ups to responses can be provided if needed. Service administrators

should provide formative feedback to trained experts to remind, teach, and encourage them to adhere to service policies and procedures. Additional suggestions are to collaborate with other AskA services to offer peer review and to run responses against a link-checking application to assure suggested Websites are accessible to the user.

10. **Provides Access to Related Information**—Besides offering direct response to user questions, digital reference services should offer access to supporting resources and information. Services can provide access to information on their content areas including an archive of previously-asked questions and answers (with users' identifiers removed), Frequently Asked Questions (FAQs) or links to external resources. Selection policies should be posted on the Website to indicate criteria for selection of external resources; these resources should be reviewed and updated regularly to ensure that content is accurate and links and references are active.

11. **Publicize**—Services providing information to the K–12 community are responsible for informing potential users of the value that can be gained from use of the service. A well-defined public relations plan can ensure that services are well publicized and promoted on a regular basis. A publicity plan may include some of the following methods: promotional messages to appropriate electronic discussion groups (e.g., listservs) and on the service Website; links to the service from related Websites; direct postal mailings to potential users; articles in print publications and press releases; and presentations at conferences and meetings. Publicity efforts should be in balance with service resources so as to avoid an inundation of questions that could overwhelm the service.

EVOLUTION OF CRITERIA

It is helpful to review the various versions of the quality criteria over time. The revisions to the "Facets of Quality" document reflect items considered important and generalizable across a growing and diverse group of digital reference services. Table 1

Table 1. Comparison between original and current criteria for digital reference services

Original Criteria	Current Criteria
Authoritative	Authoritative
Accessible	Accessible
Fast	Prompt Turnaround
Sets User Expectations	Sets User Expectations
Teaching Role	Instructive
Training	Trained Information Specialists
Private	Private
Reviewed	Reviewed
Provides Access to Related Information	Provides Access to Related Information
Publicized	Publicized
Matches Good Reference Practice*	
Noncommercial*	
Interactive*	

Note: * indicates items unique to the original criteria.

compares the original and current versions of the quality criteria.

One key issue reflected in each version of the quality criteria is that any AskA service must communicate policies and other decisions to users as a way to reduce confusion throughout the process. Information that must be shared includes standard response turnaround time, authority of experts, response policy (e.g., scope of accepted questions, type of answers provided), inability to provide a response to a particular question (due to scope, policy, etc.), and any possible perspectives that may be reflected in a response (i.e., bias due to the nature of an organization). Also stressed is the importance of evaluating the overall digital reference service and its components such as staff training programs, staff performance, and service-created resources (e.g., archives, FAQs, links to external sites).

Two facets discussed in the initial version of the document, "matches good reference practice" and "noncommercial," were eliminated due to the involvement of network members whose affiliations preclude them from upholding these criteria. Some services, such as the MAD Scientist Network, offer quality service based on subject expertise and are not expected to provide the same type of information-referral response as a reference librarian. Some services, such as Ask Shamu, are affiliated with commercial organizations, although they provide valuable information.

The facet "interactive" is included in the current version of the document. It was decided that even a basic level of interactivity should be available to users, such as a Web query form to collect useful patron information.

The second version of the "Facets of Quality" document contained the item "unbiased." The issue of bias was discussed at the AskA Consortium meeting on October 13, 1999. Although library-based services often present various sides of an issue, this cannot be assumed with all AskA services. It was suggested that expertise goes hand in hand with point of view. The decision was reached that "unbiased" should not be included in the quality criteria because in some contexts, the point of view of a given service is also a value (see the previously-discussed standard "authoritative"); the AskA services within the VRD Network can add value to it by sharing their distinct perspectives.

CONCLUSION

While the VRD standards were developed with educational AskA services in mind, they are applicable to digital reference services and networks in all contexts, including libraries, government agencies, and business. Developing digital reference consortia, such as the Collaborative Digital Reference Service effort headed by the Library of Congress (see previous paper), can use the quality criteria outlined in this paper as either a standards document to be modified, or as a model on which to build new criteria.

Individual AskA services and networks are encouraged to create and uphold their own policies for responding to questions, assessing resources for inclusion on their Websites, maintaining user privacy, determining expert authority and preparedness for participation, and publicizing the service.

It is clear that there is a need for standards as digital reference evolves from a handful of AskA services and libraries offering digital reference to a common means of interacting with users. While there has been some work in technical standards for digital reference (Lankes, 1999), there is an equal need for standards of operation. This set of quality criteria is one example of how such standards can be constructed in a cross-domain environment. It is hoped that these criteria will be of use either as criteria to be adopted in growing reference consortia, or as a model for the construction of new digital reference standards.

NOTES

1. A working draft of the discussion notes is available at *www.vrd.org/panel/criteria.html*
2. The Virtual Reference Desk (VRD) is a project dedicated to the advancement of digital reference and the successful creation and operation of human-mediated, Internet-based information systems. VRD is sponsored by the United States Department of Education, with support from the White House Office of Science and Technology Policy *<www.vrd.org>*.
3. Sources for determining ADA compliance include: CAST, Inc., "Welcome to Bobby," 9 June 1999, *<www.cast.org/bobby/>* (23 November 1999) and Jim Lubin, "Accessible Web Page Design," 18 September 1999, *<www.eskimo.com/~jlubin/disabled/webdesi.htm>* (23 November 1999).
4. A source for assisting with writing privacy policies can be found at: TRUSTe, "TRUSTe: Building a Web You Can Believe In," *<http://etrust.com/>* (23 November 1999).

REFERENCES

Kasowitz, Abby S., Blythe Bennett, Lynn Bry, Martha Dexter, Peter Milbury, Joan Stahl, Robin Summers, Steve Weimar, and Ken Williams. 1999. Facets of Quality for K–12 Digital Reference Services [Online]. Available: *http://www.vrd.org/training/facets.html* [11 November]

Kasowitz, Abby S., Blythe A. Bennett, and R. David Lankes. 2000. "Quality Standards for Digital Reference Consortia." *Reference and User Services Quarterly* 39, no. 4 (Summer): 355–63.

Lankes, R. David. 1998. *Building & Maintaining Internet Information Services: K–12 Digital Reference Services.* Syracuse, N.Y.: ERIC Clearinghouse on Information and Technology.

Lankes, R. David. 1999. The Virtual Reference Desk: Question Interchange Profile [Online]. Available: *www.vrd.org/Tech/QuIP/1.01/QuIP1.01d.PDF* [23 November].

Part III

Managing Digital Reference Services

OVERVIEW

The papers included in this section answer many questions asked by information professionals who are thinking about, or have recently started, digital reference services. Representing academic, government, and private digital reference operations, the authors thoughtfully address issues of growth, intellectual property rights, and system management. The systems used as examples have been in place for a significant period of time and have weathered many challenges and undergone many transformations.

The authors trace the evolution of several digital reference services and discuss staffing, network distribution, system infrastructure development, and the processing of large amounts of information. The systems described range from local e-mail and Web-based services on an academic campus to large international systems offering service to the public at large and using volunteer information providers.

Managing Growth for AskA Services

Pauline Lynch

This paper provides an overview of AskERIC, a personalized Internet-based service providing education information to teachers, librarians, counselors, administrators, parents, and others throughout the world. The introduction outlines several AskERIC milestones. Staffing is addressed in the second section, including the distributed network of information specialists, information resources, and technology considerations. The third section covers the AskERIC Question & Answer (Q&A) process and tools, including standardizing responses through creation of a systemwide guide, as well as a diagram of the Q&A process. Publicity methods (conference exhibits, electronic discussion groups, brochures, and a Website banner) are described in this section. The conclusion offers points to consider in building a Q&A service.

INTRODUCTION

AskERIC is a personalized Internet-based service providing education information to teachers, librarians, counselors, administrators, parents, and others throughout the United States and the world.

AskERIC is a special project of the ERIC Clearinghouse on Information & Technology, which is part of the Educational Resources Information Center (ERIC). ERIC is comprised of 16 subject-specific clearinghouses, 11 adjunct clearinghouses, and four support components. AskERIC is sponsored by the United

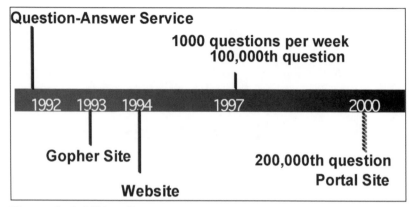

Figure 1. AskEric milestones

States Department of Education, Syracuse University, and Sun Microsystems.

The service began in 1992 and has reached several milestones. These milestones are outlined in Figure 1.

AskERIC serves over 1,000 users per week during peak times of the year. The service continues to grow in question load and staff. The following sections will highlight some of the key areas in which we have invested a significant amount of time and resources as a result of continued growth.

STAFF

Overview

In 1992, AskERIC began with two full-time staff members (see Figure 2). The question load was approximately 200 questions a week. By 1999, the question load quadrupled and the staff had expanded to over 50 including seven in-house staff and over 40 from other ERIC Clearinghouses and organizations around the country (see Figure 3).

Distributed Network of Information Specialists

Staff growth was necessary due to the increasing number of questions received. There were two options. We could increase

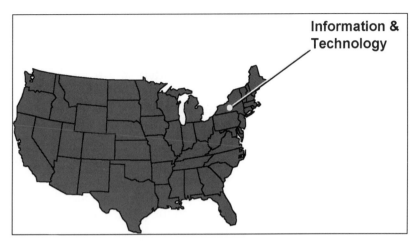

Figure 2. Location of two full-time staff at the ERIC Clearinghouse on Information & Technology

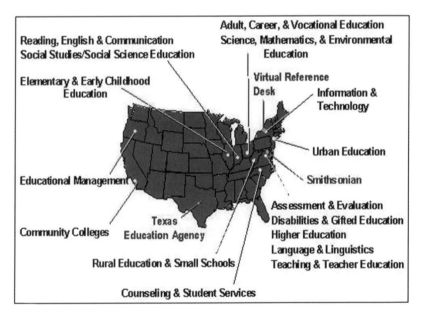

Figure 3. Map of ERIC clearinghouses and other organizations answering AskERIC questions

staff at our clearinghouse or invite the rest of the ERIC system to participate. Due to the wide range of subject-specific questions, it made the most sense to expand our expertise base along with increasing staff. Therefore we added staff from the ERIC system.

Expanding our service's subject expertise has proven beneficial for the user as well as the service. However, there are issues to contend with in a virtual work environment. The first issue is communication. Our service has found that e-mail is the most effective way to communicate with each other.

We also have an annual meeting called the AskERIC Summit. This meeting is designed to exchange ideas, determine and review policy, and look to the future. We have found that it makes it much easier to contact other staff members for assistance after meeting them in person.

The second issue to contend with is management. Each clearinghouse has its own management system, so the AskERIC coordinator coordinates staff but does not directly manage each detail. This results in a more creative and customized process.

Resources

With an increase in staff, AskERIC reorganized its internal information resources. Information resources used in responding to questions have evolved from a shared collection of bookmarks to a Website of over 1,000 resources, including Internet sites, discussion groups, archives, and full responses. Centralizing this aspect has allowed for more time to answer questions instead of conducting the redundant searches.

AskERIC also must consider the variety of technology used by participating clearinghouses. This must be taken into account whenever policy or procedures are enacted. Aside from accommodating different technology of clearinghouse staff, AskERIC has always considered technological capabilities of its users.

Q&A PROCESS & TOOLS

Standardizing Responses

The *AskERIC Systemwide Guide* was created in 1994 for a number of reasons. The main reason was to document policy and procedure that was agreed upon at the AskERIC Summits. This in turn helped with training of new staff. The most common components of responses to users and general policy were all in writing and could be referred to during training.

The guide also helped to eliminate user confusion. Users were occasionally confused by the layout of responses because each clearinghouse created their own version of response layout. With the guide, the responses became more standardized. This helped to eliminate the confusion, while still allowing for personalization within a framework.

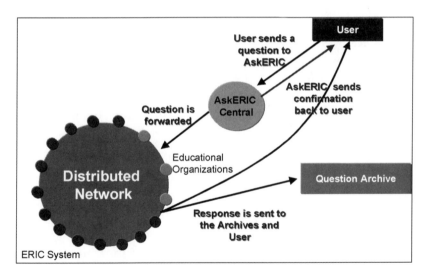

Figure 4. Current AskERIC Q/A process

AskERIC Q&A Process

Our current process is illustrated in Figure 4. Questions are received from the user at the central AskERIC office. A message is sent back to the user to let him or her know that we have received his or her question and it is being forwarded on to be answered. At the same time, the question is forwarded to an information specialist. A response is later sent back to the user with a copy forwarded to the question archives.

Areas that we are looking to automate include: statistical analysis, message forwarding, tracking messages, and archiving. Currently, we count each message sent to an information specialist by date manually. We queue groups of messages and then send all the messages out at one time. We would like to combine these steps into one. Tracking messages is also a manual process. When we receive follow-up messages or thank you messages, we must conduct a search in our e-mail package to try to find the original message. We search by e-mail, subject line, and other items. We would like to be able to pair associated messages together for future reference. At the moment, this is not possible. Finally, archiving is another cumbersome task. We have recently created an internal archive of responses. We would like to create a public archive. Therefore, we are looking for options that would allow us to strip away personal information relatively easily.

PUBLICITY

As we have grown, we have seen periods where the question load has leveled off. We are constantly trying to reach as many users as we can, which means an increase at some level. We have found that a steady slow increase is the most manageable and easiest to plan for. We have tried four methods of publicity.

The first of these is exhibiting and attending conferences. This is something that we have always done and results in a small increase in questions immediately following the conference. It does not seem to increase question load over a long period of time.

The second publicity tactic we tried was advertising to relevant electronic discussion groups. This method resulted in a small increase over a several month period.

The third was including AskERIC brochures in publication orders that went out of the ERIC Clearinghouse on Information & Technology. It seems that this increased our question load moderately for several months.

The fourth was placing a banner on our Website that stated, "Got an Education Question? AskERIC (click here)." Our Website receives approximately 2,000,000 hits per week at peak times of the year. When a banner was placed on our site in September 1997, our question load for the week was tripled. This growth was so dramatic that we removed it within a few days.

CONCLUSION

At AskERIC, we have learned a tremendous amount about growth in many aspects of our service. If your organization is considering expanding digital reference services or just beginning to build a new digital reference service, there are four points to take into consideration.

The first is to establish a solid organizational structure. This may mean one or more of the following:

- Stable staff/volunteer structure
- Standard guidelines/procedures
- Structured process for digital reference

The second point is to start out small. If possible, start out with a controlled user base. For example, this may mean offering service to five states, before making it available to the entire country. This will help you assess the strengths and weaknesses of the service, before you must deal with the demands of a heavy question load.

The third point ties in to the second. Once you have decided that you are able to handle more, a gradual increase is best. Even if you have a large staff and feel you are ready, there are issues that come with an increase that must be worked out. A large increase, all at once, will not allow you an adequate amount of time to adjust processes and procedures effectively.

The final point is to beware of publicity. Publicity is a tricky act. You are never quite sure what is going to work and what will not. To complicate things even more, it is hard to predict how well it will work and for how long. Publicity tactics should be tested on small subsets to gain an understanding of what the results might be.

Growth brings many challenges and opportunities. As AskERIC continues to grow new challenges will continue to arise, calling for further evaluation and planning in order to keep providing quality service to every user of our service.

Designing a Virtual Reference Desk: Intellectual Property Considerations*

Brett Butler

This paper presents intellectual property issues in the context of digital reference service. It introduces AnswerBase, a collaborative reference publishing service that creates a database of questions and answers. Topics include taxonomies of digital reference answers and intellectual property rightsholders, issues involving answers and owners, the concept of "fair digital use," the influence of the entertainment industry on intellectual property law, risk assessment and management, and ways to protect content and services.

INTRODUCTION, ASSUMPTIONS, AND PERSPECTIVE

The term "digital reference" can be used in many ways, but here it is discussed in the context of extended library service, not a Web vision of automated knowbots.

Digital reference is meant to include both *direction*, or guidance, and *delivery*, or presentation of the desired answer, insofar as possible and practical. This differs from the common operation of "library reference" as a directional service guiding readers to sources on the shelves.

Professional library staff maintain a goal of delivering accurate, timely, unopinionated, and high-quality reference re-

---

* The author thanks Marti West, Dick Goodman, and Chet Grycz for critical reviews.

sponses. This entails a heavy reliance on established, reviewed, quality resources from professional publishers as well as judicious use of the chaotic but fascinating resources on the Web.

Professional information publishing will not disappear with the explosive growth of Websites. Online Computer Library Center (OCLC) has just reported results of a study that identified some 3.6 million sites on the Web, defined 2.2 million as publicly available, and then noted that 25,000 sites contain 50 percent of the Web's content.[1] The September 1999 issue of *Searcher* featured an article by Larry Krumenaker documenting the sparse presence of research journals on open Websites in the midst of this "infomercial" explosion.

Libraries have traditionally provided their public services without charge, but they have never operated their acquisitions departments without cost; this model will not change because of the Web. Infour is investing in this vision in its creation of AnswerBase, the first collaborative reference publishing service, which will create a database of quality questions and answers. AnswerBase intends to be the resource of first choice for digital reference services, a component of any virtual reference desk and a building block of the collaborative digital reference service vision pioneered by the Library of Congress.

We also posit that while public domain information will grow, no broadly based public information service will be successful without including copyrighted works. If authors, publishers, and compilers continue to publish original works and information databases of value to libraries, and continue to copyright their works in order to protect their investments, intellectual property issues will exist throughout the next millennium. This paper discusses these issues in the special context of digital reference, with particular focus on the questions and answers resulting from the reference process.

A TAXONOMY OF ANSWERS

The reference process—Web-based or face-to-face—focuses on a particular kind of intellectual property and knowledge, one which is quite different from the traditional package of a book or a journal article. On the one hand, a perception might be that answers are just facts, and facts are notoriously not susceptible to copyright. At the other extreme, one legal observer has suggested one should consider that the reference *questions* themselves, if original to any degree, are subject to copyright—so we might have to consider the patrons' intellectual property rights in the development of commercial or even public reference services.

AnswerBase refers to this concept as a "knowledge bit" or "knowbit"—a combination of an inquiry and a response, linked together with human knowledge. Such knowbits may be compiled and presented as a "Q&A" item in a book, as a Frequently Asked Question (FAQ) section of a Website or listserv, or as a structured search tool in an automated help desk facility. The potential database structure is complex, but we outline here just the basic taxonomy of *answers*, which make up the core intellectual property component of a knowbit.[2]

Defining a classification by type allows us to separate distinct kinds of content. A simple taxonomy used in the AnswerBase pilot project is:

- **Fact**—A factual answer confined to the factual item itself.
- **Direct**—An answer that satisfies the question asked, adding explanation or other information to any facts provided.
- **Citation**—Reference to a resource (print or Web) that contains the answer to a question.
- **Guide**—A pathfinder or narrative providing resource references and context to guide the patron's search.
- **Referral**—General response, pointing the patron beyond specific information resources to organizations or experts.

For each of these categories, different situations exist with regard to copyrighted content.

Factual Data cannot be copyrighted, so a single "bit" of purely factual data extracted from any source, published or not, copyrighted or public domain, may be used freely. However, the compilation of data may be copyrighted so long as there is a minimal level of creativity or value added.

Direct Answers are intended to satisfy a question and may include a variety of explanatory, illustrative, discursive, or related information in addition to delivery of a specific fact, or may not include any specific facts at all. Any direct answer is subject to copyright, since it will have been created by some author, selector, or editor.

Citations provide the classic reference function—pointing the patron to an information source where a desired answer can be located. The source may be digital or print, a MARC record or a URL, or a reference to a data table in a numeric file. The descriptive part of a traditional bibliographic citation is factual, and so cannot be copyrighted. However, a typical record also involves significant intellectual effort such as classification, or added value such as review against a formal authority or value list, and as such may be individually copyrighted. Compilations are commonly copyrighted.

Guide Information is generally an intellectual work of an individual or group, although guides can be created by automated searches of copyrighted or public domain databases. Selection of recommended resources from a larger body of data is generally recognized as a value sufficient to qualify the work for copyright.

A *Referral* answer is, as with guides, a subjective evaluation made by a human within the context of a discussion, and is clearly subject to copyright. Whether the automated referral-links generated by the automated systems at Alexa (*www.alexa.com*) are copyrightable is an issue for Brewster Kahle, Alexa Internet's co-founder and president, to debate.

A TAXONOMY OF OWNERS

To understand the flow of intellectual property issues around our taxonomy of answers, we need to survey the types of intellectual property rightsholders (referred to as "owners," although in some cases they are actually licensees of primary IP holders) that may be involved in the creation and delivery of a single answer. A simple list is:

- **Author**—The original creator of the content (text, image, multimedia, etc.).

- **Publisher**—The primary organizer and distributor of the author's content.[3]
- **Selector**—One who extracts answers from publishers' content packages.
- **Editor**—One who selects answers and compiles them into further packages.
- **Compiler**—A publisher that re-organizes original answers, often adding other proprietary value (such as AnswerBase).

There are many variations of these roles, and many combinations as well, but these will serve as illustrations for our discussion here. The point is that each kind of contributor to the flow of intellectual property has a different claim upon the answer as a work (and as a component of a knowledge bit), and therefore a different relationship to the processes of digital reference.

Each owner class also has a different attitude toward protection of its intellectual property. Recognizing these differences will assist in the planning of a library's digital reference services in its risk assessment, its business management, and in its protection of its own intellectual property. Combining the characteristics of answers and owners, and recognizing the role of each in creating a "knowledge bit," we end up with a "copyright chain" (see Table 2).

Table 2 indicates intellectual property claims, and employs the © sign to indicate where an actual copyright is commonly filed. As discussed below, this distinction is important because the nominal "copyright owner" is more likely to be identifiable, and is more likely to litigate or take other action to defend copy-

Table 2. Copyright and intellectual property claims

Answers:	Author	Publisher	Selector	Editor	Compiler
Facts	None	No	No	No	No
Direct	Yes	Yes:©	No	No	Licensed
Citation	No	No	Yes	No	Yes: ©
Guide	Yes	Yes:©	No	No	Licensed
Referral	Yes: ©	No	No	No	Licensed

right, even though authors, selectors, editors, and compilers may in fact have a legal interest.

It should be noted that a recent *National Writers Union* decision as cited in the *Wall Street Journal,* 28 September 1999, gives authors a stronger voice in e-publishing matters, ruling that "publishers can't put freelance articles online and onto CD-ROMs without permission from writers." In the past, publishers had asserted that right and distributors such as University Microfilms had presumed that publishers had such rights. The permissions picture is now much more complex; in the reference perspective, content "aggregators" such as AnswerBase may need to deal directly with authors of content such as encyclopedia chapters, rather than with the original print or media publishers.

ISSUES WITH ANSWERS AND OWNERS

Because of the virtual distribution capability of the Internet, low-cost use can be made of even minute sections of traditional print packages—an illustration, a table, a text paragraph—at the same time that it is becoming practical to ship a digital edition of a 300-page book to a retail bookstore for local printing.

Publishers not accustomed to selling chapters of their books, or individual articles from their journals, now face demand from Web-based buyers and information aggregators to do so. For reference publishers, the opportunity to sell, for instance, a few names or paragraphs from a directory or compilation is offset by the concern that the unused portion of that data will no longer be bought by the library for its reference shelf. The forays of directory publishers into "legacy" online services such as DIALOG in the 1980s were not successful, because the income obtained from a quick "item" search was not sufficient to offset the costs of preparation and the risk of losing subscriptions.

Today, however, both libraries and traditional information publishers are challenged by the explosive growth of a wide variety of free reference services on the Web—an environment in which more people search Excite (*www.excite.com*) every day than use DIALOG in a year. This situation has led to increased awareness among reference librarians of the need to become more proactive in offering quality electronic reference service over the Web, as illustrated by the initiatives of the Virtual Reference Desk Project and the Collaborative Digital Reference Service vision championed by the Library of Congress.

At the same time, there is an increasing awareness among at least some publishers that the opportunity to present their content openly on the Web now exceeds the risk of allowing access to their reference content. While a controlled-subscription model will predominate for some time, some scholarly publishers such as Annual Reviews are now offering chapter or article content on a per-request basis. Other publishers are offering the first chapter or other extracts of their works for free through electronic booksellers, using a sample of content to stimulate the sale of their publications. AnswerBase is aiming to organize an equitable combination of a base subscription offering free content and access to purchase or license of more extensive "answers."

There are three main issues which must be resolved before electronic reference can grow in a manner which will allow expert library reference to compete with Web alternatives. These concern "fair digital use" (FDU), mutually assured protection, and free vs. fee philosophies.

"Fair Digital Use" (FDU)

It is important to recognize that "fair use," a set of guidelines most libraries believe direct their use and re-use of works on their shelves, is a print-world concept which has neither been tested nor litigated in the electronic world.

The library and publishing communities are attempting to define a concept of "fair digital use" in an environment that, because of the explosive growth of Web-based e-commerce, has higher stakes than was previously the case with copying print works. For instance, the University of California is trying to prevent a company called Versity.com from transcribing class notes in professors' classes and then publishing them on a free Website, according to the *San Francisco Chronicle*, 2 October 1999.

Focusing on a "fair use" set of electronic guidelines will not be productive, because such agreements are extremely complex and fragile, and do not have much effect unless based on litigation and a court decision. The speed of e-commerce will not mix well with another generation's reprise of the *Williams and Wilkins* case.

Rather, we believe strongly that contract and license law guidelines will evolve, drawing on open market competition among information publishers for library budgets, that will create an ad hoc definition of "fair digital use" (FDU). The growth of cooperative library negotiating efforts, led by such groups as OhioLink, has actually improved the overall situation for both libraries and publishers (at least in the cases where negotiations do not turn simply on pricing).

Mutually Assured Protection

Mutually assured protection is a goal that publishers and librarians can now hold in common—the defense of quality information against the "barbarians at the gate" on the Web. The loss of quality publishing processes is all too obvious at numerous Websites that purport to offer advice, guidance, and reference information. These services know nothing of knowledge that is not found on the Web—the contents of the books sold by Amazon.com are not even searchable by Excite or Yahoo!.

Over the past two decades, it seemed that libraries and publishers were heading on a slow, downward spiral where prices would keep rising and sales would keep decreasing, providing less information to fewer people. This is referred to by the nuclear warriors as "mutually assured destruction." This was particularly true in the area of scholarly scientific journals, but was a factor in all kinds of reference publishing. Now, however, the market outreach newly provided by the Web coupled with low actual costs of distribution allows both libraries and publishers to reach out to a larger audience while supporting each other.

With courage and a vision based on growth rather than defending a shrinking market, libraries and publishers can assure each other's protection against the worrisome vision of "bad information driving out good."

Free vs. Fee Philosophies

Free vs. fee philosophies have been another battleground for publishers and libraries. As previously mentioned, libraries have traditionally provided their public services without charge, but they have never operated their acquisitions departments without cost. At the same time, their services have been defined and limited in ways that no longer meet the expectations of Web-aware consumers and computer-trained students. In an environment where every library Internet terminal now provides the library patron with an advertising-supported free information service, the traditional rules no longer apply.

We can expect to see new, creative models for combining library-supported free service to patrons with fee-based sales activities. AnswerBase will, for instance, point to a local library catalog where a particular book is recommended as a response to an inquiry, but will also give the patron the option of ordering the book from a local bookstore or the publisher. Income from these referrals will help keep subscription prices reasonable. We are also exploring the potential of offering two editions: one for the traditional content service alone and another lower-cost subscription including selected advertising.

THE ENTERTAINMENT ENVIRONMENT

It is important to recognize, as librarians and professional publishers face digital copyright, digital fair use, and licensing issues, that much of the legal context in which we will be operating is effectively being driven by the entertainment industry. There are much larger issues of intellectual property protection operating in the television, movie, music, and game businesses than in the mass-market newspaper and magazine industries. Professional publishing, particularly reference information, isn't even on the agenda of the firms, lobbyists, and legislators creating copyright legislation.

The recent extension of copyright was not pushed through Congress to deprive libraries of the opportunity to convert scholarly works from print to digital for another twenty years;

it was widely attributed in the press to the Disney Corporation's desire to protect its rights in the Mickey Mouse character into the new millennium.

The law, and the rhetoric of discussions that surround it, is intended more so to protect movie and music publishers from illegal copying of CD and DVD editions of their works than scholarly publishing interests. The behavior of publishers and librarians in this specialized environment of information publishing should not be driven by the entertainment and Internet industries' agenda.

One current example of this is the recent move by eBay Inc. to forbid a company called AuctionWatch.com from compiling searches of eBay auction offerings and those of its competitors into a single evaluation site, as reported in the *San Francisco Chronicle*, 30 September 1999.

RISK ASSESSMENT AND MANAGEMENT

Libraries planning to offer electronic reference services can expect to face a complex and unclear legal position for the next decade or more. One cannot expect publishers, as represented by their trade associations, to take moderate or compromising positions on the protection of their intellectual property. Lawyers and institutional managers will always recommend erring on the side of conservatism. Nobody will provide a fixed set of guidelines for acquiring and using electronic reference information. (AnswerBase's solution will be to acquire specific licenses for the use of any content captured by itself or its contributor libraries.)

For independent efforts, one must perform a risk assessment of one's service unless specific permissions, rights, or licenses are acquired for all intended uses of any digital (or digitally converted) information in a Web or network distribution environment.

Having proposed that the classic formulation of "fair use" is not fixed in place for cyberspace, we nonetheless would use the main points of its guidelines. Here is a discussion of these tenets by Condoleezza Rice, former provost of Stanford University (the discussion is available at *http://fairuse.stanford.edu/*

rice.html, a site that is an excellent resource of "fair use" information and debate).

This memorandum provides a general description of the applicability of the copyright law and the so-called "fair use" exemptions to the copyright law's general prohibition on copying. It also describes "safe harbor" guidelines applicable to classroom copying.

The federal copyright statute governs the reproduction of works of authorship. In general, works governed by copyright law include such traditional works of authorship as books, photographs, music, drama, video and sculpture, and also software, multimedia, and databases. Copyrighted works are protected regardless of the medium in which they are created or reproduced; thus, copyright extends to digital works and works transformed into a digital format. Copyrighted works are not limited to those that bear a copyright notice. As a result of changes in copyright law, works published since March 1, 1989 need not bear a copyright notice to be protected under the statute. Two provisions of the copyright statute are of particular importance to teachers and researchers: (1) provision that codifies the doctrine of "fair use," under which limited copying of copyrighted works without the permission of the owner is allowed for certain teaching and research purposes; and (2) a provision that establishes special limitations and exemptions for the reproduction of copyrighted works by libraries and archives.

The concept of fair use is necessarily somewhat vague when discussed in the abstract. Its application depends critically on the particular facts of the individual situation. Neither the case law nor the statutory law provides bright lines concerning which uses are fair and which are not. However, you may find it helpful to refer to certain third party source materials.

Guidelines for classroom copying by not-for-profit educational institutions have been prepared by a group consisting of the Authors League of America, the Association of American Publishers, and an ad hoc committee of educational institutions and organizations. In addition, fair use guidelines for educational multimedia have been prepared by a group coordinated by the consortium of College and University Multimedia Centers (CCUMC). These guidelines describe safe harbor conditions, but do not purport to define the full extent of "fair use." . . . The "fair use" doctrine allows limited reproduction of copyrighted works for educational and research purposes. The relevant portion of the copyright statute provides that the "fair use" of a copyrighted work, including reproduction "for purposes such as criticism, news reporting, teaching (including multiple copies for classroom use), scholarship, or research" is not an infringement of copyright. The law lists the following factors as the ones to be evaluated in determining whether a particular use of a copyrighted work is a permitted "fair use," rather than an infringement of the copyright:

- the purpose and character of the use, including whether such use is of a commercial nature or is for nonprofit educational purposes;
- the nature of the copyrighted work
- the amount and substantiality of the portion used in relation to the copyrighted work as a whole
- the effect of the use upon the potential market for or value of the copyrighted work.

Although all of these factors will be considered, the last factor is the most important in determining whether a particular use is "fair." Where a work is available for purchase or license from the copyright owner in the medium or format desired, copying of all or a significant portion of the work in lieu of purchasing or licensing a sufficient number of "authorized" copies would be presumptively unfair. Where only a small portion of a work is to be copied and the work would not be used if purchase or licensing of a sufficient number of authorized copies were required, the intended use is more likely to be found to be fair.[4]

This excerpt gives the context for risk assessment, and illustrates how little direction even a provost and well-known political figure can provide us. In a conclusion, Rice (1998) states, "Please note that the guidelines are intended to state the minimum, not the maximum, extent of the fair use doctrine," thus throwing the decision back to the faculty.

If one is to proceed with electronic reference without complete legal coverage—and the ability to gain this protection may not be available until the next millennium—you will need to judge the risk on the parameters highlighted below, watching changes in the actual law.

Purpose and Character of Use

In general, libraries fall squarely under the core exemptions of "teaching, scholarship, or research," although fee services may not be so viewed even though operated by a nonprofit organization. And content incorporated in commercial products is not likely to be considered within the core educational exemption.

Nature of the Copyrighted Work

This element of fair use receives less attention than the others, but is particularly related to the use of reference information or extracts of facts and answers from other works. For instance, if a directory is published as a product given to members of a professional society, its purpose is quite different from that of a commercial directory sold primarily in retail stores.

Amount and Substantiality of the Portion Used

This element is quite important in gauging the use of published information. Many factual answers will extract a very small portion of a reference work such as an almanac or guide. The demands of reference patrons are so broad that many reference works are used only occasionally to answer patrons' questions. The effect of cumulative extraction over time, if the content is compiled into an internal database and made available, however, must be determined.

Effect of Use upon the Potential Market for or Value of the Copyrighted Work

This element is important to consider in two parts: the *potential market* and the *value of* the copyrighted work.

The Potential Market Impact

It is unclear whether the consideration here is for the potential market for the existing work, or for digital editions, or versions derived from the digital work. Rice (1998) states (bold type added by author), "Where a work is available for purchase or license from the copyright owner **in the medium or format desired**, copying of all or a significant portion of the work in lieu of purchasing or licensing a sufficient number of 'authorized' copies would be preemptively unfair. Where only a small portion of a work is to be copied and the work would not be used if purchase or licensing of a sufficient number of authorized copies were required, the intended use is more likely to be found to be fair."

The author has added the bold highlighting to the portion of the comment, which suggests that converting a print work is more acceptable if a digital format is not available. It is not clear what the position of this effort is in law. In any case, it is not the present market but the potential market that must be considered.

The language and intent clearly imply that any review of a specific "fair use" activity must consider the negative impact of the action on a potential market. It has not been considered that such actions might have a positive impact as well, which would mitigate any negative impacts. Since any evaluation beyond the most obvious cases of plagiarism or copying involve projecting an uncertain future, we believe both positive and negative impacts on a potential market should be considered by all parties. For instance, AnswerBase believes that extraction of a small amount of content from a publisher's work, and providing wide distribution to potential buyers coupled with an online ordering facility, might increase sales of many reference and professional works.

It would also be practical to evaluate the present and future availability of the work. For practical purposes, a book that is out of print or a journal no longer in the publisher's inventory will generate no future sales whether fair use applications exist or not. In these cases, although copyright protection exists, no loss of income is to be seen. With the new "on-demand" technology, libraries might create digital editions of works (at their expense, as needed) which could be put in a digital inventory for future sale, with appropriate royalties accruing to authors or publishers. In this case fair use enhances future markets and income potential.

The Value of the Work

Some of the considerations here are related closely to market value, but a somewhat different perspective can apply. The value of a work that is unknown, but located and made available, may be related to the tree falling silently in the forest—if nobody reads what you write, have you said anything?

The long-term value of a work can be enhanced by capture of an author's work, selection by expert librarians, addition of search and other metadata, and inclusion of it in a broadly based, widely used information database. Publishers that have already established an ongoing value for specific works will likely want to participate in the income stream of such an aggregated database.

The good news is this model is not new: when the Information Access ASAP databases on the DIALOG online system pioneered fulltext online fifteen years ago, a business model was established that was acceptable to over 1,000 publishers and supports the use of millions of professional and popular articles online today.

Although DIALOG was more of a closed system than the Web, it served thousands of large corporations in an effective manner without any active security or tracking system for more than a decade. Additional measures are being taken to provide security in a Web environment today, most recently illustrated by the initiative by Adobe to deliver a secure form of its PDF format. Professional booksellers such as Fatbrain.com will employ Adobe's system to deliver both self-authored and published content securely over the Web.

In these conditions, it is clearly a value-enhancing effort for libraries to participate in reorganization of publishers' works into forms suitable for their patrons and other Web users.

PROTECTING YOUR CONTENT AND SERVICES

If libraries and professional publishers can find accommodation in digital reference environments, it is probably partly because both institutions have a profound respect for the value of intellectual property. Libraries have always respected copyright and intellectual property, while contending about the limits of specific agreements—particularly as the uncertainties of electronic publishing have led some publishers to propose policies more restrictive than previously common.

Technology is now making it a reality that libraries themselves are becoming publishers, or at least aggregators and distributors. Much agreement has been reached between libraries and professional publishers about the terms of service to an organization's patrons, making it possible for a public library patron to consult a commercial service such as InfoTrac over the Web from home with little difficulty.

The Web environment, though, is creating some challenges because this traditional respect for copyright does not extend to all on the Web. Some observers believe, on practical or philosophical grounds, that copyright is obsolete in cyberspace. More frequently seen today, though, are cyberpirates that act as if anything on the Web is theirs. Despite controlling legislation, the practical aspects of appropriate behavior regarding others' Website data are yet very uncontrolled. This leads to interesting scenes involving litigation about linking—or not linking—one's site to another's data. When these practices reach into information sites created and operated by libraries or library-related organizations such as AskA services, major issues are created.

Those developing digital reference services in the next decade will need to be as vigilant in protecting their own or their organization's intellectual property as they will need to be respectful of others'. Even if one desires to allow open and free use, registration of copyright in digital resources and knowledge, and protection of that asset by legal means if necessary, is a precondition of public access and operation.

THE ANSWERBASE PERSPECTIVE: BEING VALUABLE

AnswerBase believes that libraries and professional publishers can work together to create digital reference services that will serve both parties. AnswerBase acts as an intermediary between the reference patron and primary information publishers. The key to gaining support—licenses, permissions, and content—from those publishers is to show them added value. Libraries do this by selecting valuable material, making it findable with search and other metadata, and recommending the publisher's work. AnswerBase is an expert compiler (or aggregator as classified by the Web markets) that enhances libraries' contributions, combines them with a critical mass of content, and markets the new combination. AnswerBase does this in an environment where both the library contributor and the publisher receive income based on their work and intellectual property rights.

These combined efforts result in new value to the publisher and author, generally in a new market and application where the publisher does not reach or in a new product package the individual publisher does not offer. It is important to realize, however, that these positive results will not be obtained through independent effort or in the atmosphere of contention often found in the past. Positive results will be obtained by creation of mutually beneficial agreements between individual publishers and individual libraries or consortia of libraries acting together.

As Ann Okerson (1999) observes in the current issue of DigiLib,

> What we have learned through LIBLICENSE, and in the negotiating fray in the last several years, is that licensing, thoughtfully approached, can be an outstanding arena for identifying very diverse needs and for bringing together the parties to craft resolution to difficult issues. It can be

argued that in some ways the information community gains advantages from working in the licensing environment, beyond those in the print world where take-it-or-leave-it pricing was governed by a copyright regime. Copyright and sale are far from obsolete—in fact strong copyright law is needed as a foundation for effective licensing—but licenses can offer new modes and opportunities to do our fundamental jobs better and thus assure the survival and prosperity of the scholarly and scientific publishing and reading communities.

Real progress in digital reference intellectual property will occur at the meeting table, with specific proposals coupled with explicit agreements. This is a large job, because there is no central clearinghouse where blanket agreements exist, but a critical mass of information can be achieved by these means.

SUMMARY

Digital reference services are in some sense on the cutting edge of intellectual property law and practice in libraries, at least if digital reference is understood to include providing actual answers. Because of the expectations of instant service raised by such commercial services as Ask Jeeves (askjeeves.com) and About.com (on the Web, you will get some answer immediately), mere directional reference services are not likely to extend libraries' service offerings to the level desired.

The more ambitious goal of initiatives such as the Library of Congress Collaborative Digital Reference Service effort is to provide live, networked access to a real reference librarian—a level of expertise and knowledge and communication not achieved with e-mail based reference or the use of volunteer experts such as those found on chat groups and some commercial services. This kind of service will need to depend on a core archive or database of frequently asked or popular questions and answers in order to avoid being overwhelmed with inquiries.

Because these visions of reference service embody the values and approach of the academic or public library reference desk—to answer any question at any time—these visions will need to use an extremely broad range of sources of facts and answers. An answer of any intellectual content is a knowledge bit subject to copyright. If used in a Web environment, and subject to further distribution beyond the initial answer, digital reference services will be inextricably intertwined with intellectual property issues.

NOTES

1. See *www.oclc.org/oclc/research/projects/webstats/*.
2. The "knowbit" itself, comprised of query, answer, and metadata such as classification, is a compilation and subject to individual copyright if anybody were to desire to file.
3. The author may, of course, be the publisher, a path being encouraged by such Web distributors as Fatbrain.com, with its E-Matter author-to-reader Web service.
4. Printed with permission from Stanford University.

REFERENCES

Okerson, Ann. 1999. "The LIBLICENSE Project and How It Grows." *D-Lib Magazine* 5, no. 9. Available: *www.dlib.org/dlib/september99/okerson/09okerson.html* (Accessed 16 March 2000).

Rice, Condoleezza. 1998. "Copyright and Fair Use: Stanford University Libraries." [Online]. Available: *http://fairuse.stanford.edu/rice.html* (Accessed 26 April 2000).

Simple and Sophisticated Methods for Processing Large Volumes of Question and Answer Information through the World Wide Web

Lynn Bry

The MAD Scientist Network (www.madsci.org) is a Web-based Ask-A-Scientist service with more than four years experience in handling questions from the K–12 community and general public. It is a volunteer organization staffed and run by more than 800 scientists from locations around the globe. A constant consideration over the course of the service's evolution has involved developing means for handling an increasing volume of questions. The service has found that a combination of simple techniques, such as manipulating the design of the Website, and more sophisticated ones, including the development of software for processing questions and answers, has allowed the service to effectively respond to the majority of questions received. This paper discusses both simple and sophisticated methods that can be implemented by other services, and provides an overview of functions that can be automated by Common Gateway Interface (CGI) scripts.

INTRODUCTION

The MAD Scientist Network (MADSci) started in 1995 as a Web-based entity at Washington University Medical School in St. Louis where local K–12 students could ask questions of scientists at the medical school. We have grown from a service of

40 volunteers, answering questions in chemistry and the biological sciences, to one with more than 800 volunteer scientists who answer questions in subjects from Astronomy to Zoology. In addition, our online, searchable archive stores more than 12,000 question/answer pairs and provides an added resource for our visitors and staff.

Traffic through our site has markedly increased since our inception and, as expected, so have the number of questions received. Currently we attract between a quarter to half a million visitors a month and receive over 3,000 questions in the same time period. Our overall response rate to questions is 91 percent, or 95 percent when it is possible to contact the person who asked the question.[1]

Our existence as a Web-based entity offers a number of advantages for receiving and answering an ever growing number of questions:

- The global availability of the Web lets users and staff interact with material on our site regardless of where they physically reside.
- The service is available 24 hours a day, 7 days a week. Questions and answers may be submitted and processed at any time.
- Interfaces can be designed and constructed in a platform-independent manner. Those viewing or who are involved in reviewing material do not require a specific system, Web browser, or special software.
- The use of Common Gateway Interface (CGI) scripts[2] and other tools allows processing of questions and answers before any direct human intervention. In many instances this form of "triage" greatly streamlines the process of providing answers to a large number of questions, but comes at the price of requiring local expertise in the area of CGI programming.

Since our inception, we have developed software into a package called Moderator. The package handles the processing of questions and answers and assumes many of the repetitive and "mundane" tasks associated with maintaining our site.

Some of these tasks include:

- Formatting questions and answers with hypertext.
- Creating views of specific sets of files in our archives.
- Tracking the progress and "history" of questions sent to experts.
- Archiving files and updating the search engine.

Further information about the organization of our site, and the Moderator software developed to maintain the MAD Scientist Network may be found at: MadSci Information Desk: *www.madsci.org/info.html* and Ask-An-Expert Resources: *www.madsci.org/ask_expert*.

ORGANIZATION AND STRATIFICATION OF PERSONNEL

Figure 5 demonstrates the organization of personnel involved in the MAD Scientist Network, particularly the stratification that allows us to distribute the answering of questions among a large number of people. We rely on an infrastructure of Web-based,

Figure 5: Organization of personnel involved in the MAD Scientist Network

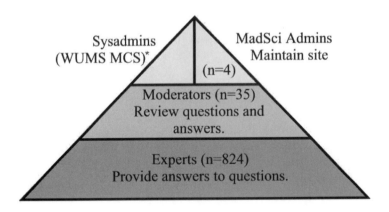

*WUMS MCS = Washington University Medical School Medical Computing Staff

CGI interfaces to facilitate the distribution of this workload. In this manner only a few individuals need be involved in networking, programming, Web design, and system administration, leaving our scientists to do what they do best: answer questions. Individuals participating in our site are subdivided into four groups: experts, moderators, MADSci administrators, and system administrators.

Experts

The expert represents an end-point for obtaining specific information to answer a question. Given that this role is the most basic and time consuming part of locating an answer, we distribute the work among the greatest number of people. Scientists wishing to answer questions sign-up through an online form at: *www.madsci.org/join/*

Experts' required skills include the ability to use e-mail and a Web browser, and expertise in one or more subjects. They require no knowledge of HTML, a particular operating system, or a programming language. An introduction sent to new experts, and an online manual (*www.madsci.org/ans/manual.html*) provide a guide and expectations for answering questions.

Moderators

Moderators review questions and answers, and direct questions to specific scientists. This trafficking function serves to direct questions as specifically as possible to qualified experts. Most moderators have answered 25 or more questions as "experts" and so have previous experience with the process. In addition, moderators must have advanced knowledge (graduate student or higher) of their areas of review. Contact with the MadSci administrators, and an online manual provide information about the tasks to be performed (*www.madsci.org/ask_expert/ manual.html*). No knowledge of UNIX (on which the MadSci site operates) is required.

MadSci Administrators

These individuals answer mail, maintain the Web server and deal with issues related to the site. Knowledge of UNIX and HTML are required. Most have experience programming in Perl (a scripted programming language commonly used for CGI programming), the language used to develop the Moderator package.

System Administrators

The system administrators in the medical library oversee the MadSci machine as part of the computer hub at Washington University Medical School. They perform regular backups, software upgrades, and handle networking and security issues concerning our site.

ASKING QUESTIONS

A number of techniques, some very simple and others more sophisticated, can greatly improve the efficiency of an AskA service in handling a large number of inquiries.

1. Rather than keep an Ask-An-Expert function hidden, display the function, but use it to lead users through materials and methods that can help them find answers on their own.
2. For questions that arrive at your site, use CGI scripts or other forms of Web software to filter and potentially direct questions to specific resources.
3. Archive your collected question/answer information, and make it searchable. As illustrated below, an online archive provides a valuable resource both for users and for staff involved in answering and processing questions.

MADSci incorporates these techniques by making it easy to ask a question; leading users through materials and methods that can help them find an answer; using CGI scripts to process and triage information before it is read by human eyes; and enabling users to ask questions even if they lack an e-mail address.

Make It Easy to Ask a Question

Asking questions forms the basis of the MAD Scientist Network. An ASK icon at the bottom of every page allows visitors to submit questions. However, if even 1 percent of visitors asked a single question, our ability to respond to most, if not all, inquiries would become increasingly difficult! We have implemented a series of checks to filter the questions that ultimately require an answer from a scientist.

Lead Users through Materials and Methods That Can Help Them Find an Answer

Figure 6 illustrates how arrangement of pages and use of CGI scripts reduces the number of questions requiring review and direct answering. On average, 17,000 visitors a month access the page prefacing the "Ask-A-Question" form <*www.madsci.org/ submit.html*> (4–5 percent of all total visitors).

This prefacing page encourages users to check existing resources and lists types of questions the service will not answer. From this page 52 percent of users jump to other locations on *www.madsci.org*, while 48 percent progress to the page for submitting questions.[3] From here, nearly half submit a question (22 percent of the original number of users). After questions are processed by software on the site, a percentage of questions await review by one of the MadSci moderators. Though this second tier of review by computer software succeeds in finding answers to questions from only 3–4 percent of total users, it represents 15–20 percent of the questions that would otherwise require active review and processing by our staff.

We implemented the "prefacing page" in early 1997 and monitored the number of questions that arrived there over the next two months. We found that this page dropped our question load by about 50 percent, as it does to this day. The majority of questions "answered" by this method involved cases where the MadSci moderators would have otherwise directed

Figure 6. Illustration of the paths users may follow when asking questions

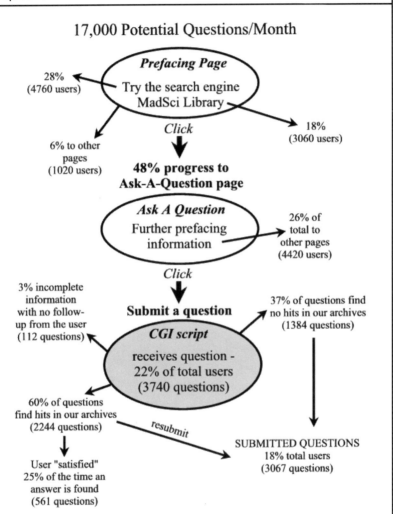

17,000 Potential Questions/Month

Prefacing Page
Try the search engine
MadSci Library

28%
(4760 users)

18%
(3060 users)

Click

6% to other pages
(1020 users)

48% progress to Ask-A-Question page

Ask A Question
Further prefacing information

26% of total to other pages
(4420 users)

Click

3% incomplete information with no follow-up from the user
(112 questions)

Submit a question

37% of questions find no hits in our archives
(1384 questions)

CGI script
receives question - 22% of total users
(3740 questions)

60% of questions find hits in our archives
(2244 questions)

resubmit

SUBMITTED QUESTIONS
18% total users
(3067 questions)

User "satisfied" 25% of the time an answer is found
(561 questions)

Approximately 18 percent of individuals progressing through this process will eventually submit a question to be reviewed by the MadSci moderators. Information in this figure is based on statistics from September 1999 where 17,112 passes across the page at *www.madsci.org/submit.html* were recorded and tracked. User "sessions" were followed by assigning Apache Webserver cookies, and analyzing sessions in the server log. Though the tracking indicates the links users followed, it does not indicate their intent to ask a question during the process.

users to files in our archives, the MadSci Library, or to existing Web resources that could answer their questions. This single action enabled us to focus more specifically on questions lacking immediate answers.[4]

Though this method makes the user's ultimate goal of asking a question one or more clicks away, it serves the users of the site, who may obtain immediate answers, and helps the staff by reducing the load of incoming questions.

Use CGI Scripts to Process and Triage Information before It Is Read by Human Eyes

Our question form prompts users for their name, e-mail address, grade level and location, though only a question and "area of science" need be entered. When submitted, software in the Moderator package performs a number of checks to verify whether:

- The user entered a question and area of science.
- The question is at least three words long.
- E-mail addresses (if entered) have the format *user@some.host* as well as a valid domain name.

The software then compares the question against the MadSci Archives at *www.madsci.org/circumnav/* to locate existing answers. If found, the user receives a list of links with the option of resubmitting his or her question. Approximately 63 percent of questions are matched with archived files. On average, only 25 percent of users deem their questions answered by this process (15 percent of all submitted questions). If the question found no hits, or is resubmitted, it then becomes available for review by the MadSci moderators.

Ability to Ask Questions Even If Users Lack an E-mail Address

We do not require users to provide an e-mail address should they lack one or simply wish to submit a question anonymously. The Moderator package generates a unique ID number for each question. After sending a question to our site, the user receives a Web page with the ID number and a link to our status page (*www.madsci.org/status.html*) with the ID number filled in. This page may be bookmarked, allowing a user to check his or her question when desired. In addition, users who lack or do not wish to submit their e-mail address may follow a question's progress. The function allows some users to edit their questions if they did not pass review and minimizes the amount of mail to the main account concerning the status of questions.

MODERATORS: QUESTION AND ANSWER REVIEW

We consider the review of questions and answers an important process. Question review allows us to more rapidly respond to inquiries and keeps our experts from having to deal with questions answered in our archives or by materials the user could find locally or on the World Wide Web. We also use the review process to contact users so they may clarify their questions before we send them to experts. On average, only 30–40 percent of questions pass review and are sent to a scientist for an answer. The process plays an equally important role in checking the accuracy of information in the answers we receive.

The Moderator package provides a Web-based interface for reviewing questions and answers. It gives moderators the tools needed to direct a question to the best expert available to answer it. The interface may be accessed 24 hours a day. It functions in any forms-capable browser and relies on a series of simple point and click actions.

We assign moderators specific subjects relative to their areas of expertise. Moderators have the following options when reviewing files:

- Answer a question directly.
- Post a question and answer to public or to private Web space.
- Notify the user by e-mail (if address provided) if more information is needed or we are not able to answer the question, or where the user can look for an answer.
- Send a question to an expert for an answer.
- Forward the question to another AskA service (e.g., Virtual Reference Desk).

- Change the area of science (e.g., from Earth Sciences to Astronomy).
- Edit a question or answer.
- Place an answer "on hold" and notify the expert of changes to be made.
- Notify experts of outstanding questions, assign "delinquencies" if no response was ever provided, and recycle the question to send it to another expert.
- Delete a question or answer from the queue.

The system provides notification to those involved in asking or answering a question when an e-mail address is available. Moderators may alter messages to suit specific situations. In addition, the system tracks the progress of reviewed questions, maintains statistics on experts, and provides a function whereby moderators can grade the quality of answers from experts.

EXPERT: ANSWERING A QUESTION

Our ability to answer a large number of queries in a detailed manner depends largely on our knowledge base of scientists. As with asking a question, we also try to make answering one as easy as possible.

Experts receive questions by e-mail and have the option to answer or defer them. The message includes URLs for both options. With a single click, the experts log into the online interface if their mail program links to the Web. Separate instructions list a direct URL if this is not the case. The answer interface provides a number of options including:

- Defer the question so it may be recycled and sent to another expert.
- Upload images with an answer (supports GIF, JPEG, BMP, and TIFF).
- Allow experts to use their own hypertext formatting in an answer.
- Preview an answer before submitting it.

ARCHIVING AND SEARCH FUNCTIONS

Any AskA service should organize its collected question and answer information into a searchable archive. Privacy issues dictate that certain question-answer pairs, and elements of other files (names and e-mail addresses, for instance) should not be made available on the Web. However, filters and other means can be devised that allow the remaining information to be placed in public Web space or within a protected area.

In this day and age anyone can create a searchable archive at low to no cost. Sites such as AltaVista (*www.altavista.com*) allow users to enter the URL of directories and pages they wish to have indexed (*www.altavista.com/cgi-bin/query?pg=addurl*). Functions within the AltaVista search engine then allow you to search these files. For instance, a query of "dinosaurs +host:www.madsci.org" at AltaVista locates files about dinosaurs on *www.madsci.org*. The "+host:www.madsci.org" in the query can be incorporated within a search form on a site allowing users to specifically search through the material on a site (*doc.altavista.com/business_solutions/search_link/add_avsearch. shtml*). For a comparison of the information located, you can try a search for dinosaurs at the MADSci search engine, which uses the Glimpse package (*www.madsci.org/MS_search.html*). In addition to the added files a user is likely to find with the MADSci search engine, freely available packages such as Glimpse allow sites to develop integrated functions to suit the needs of users, experts and administrators. Glimpse is used on the MADSci Website to perform auto-answering of questions with material from our archives, and to search our archives relative to grade level and subject area.

SUMMARY

A variety of techniques can be used to process and distinguish which questions require the involvement of an expert to obtain an answer. Designing information on Web pages to direct users to existing resources increases the user's ability to find an immediate answer and also allows sites with limited staff to focus their efforts on queries not necessarily answered by available information. This form of "question triage" is perhaps the easiest to implement, requiring alterations in the layout of Web pages. For sites with an extensive knowledge base, stratification of personnel can allow effective trafficking of questions to qualified experts by a small number of "moderators" who review questions and direct them appropriately.

More sophisticated methods invariably involve the use of CGI scripts and local knowledge of a programming language. However, as a second tier of triaging questions, it provides a more direct means of locating information that can potentially answer a user's question.

APPENDIX

Software & Hardware Used by the MAD Scientist Network

Hardware: SUN Ultra2 Server (*www.madsci.org*)
Operating System: Solaris (UNIX)
Webserver: Apache 1.3.9 server (*www.apache.org/*)
CGI Programming: Perl 5.004 (*www.perl.com/*)
Search Engine: Glimpse 4.1 (*http://glimpse.cs.arizona.edu/*)
Additional Software & Utilities:
   mod_perl (*http://perl.apache.org/*): Speed performance of perl CGI scipts.
   GDBM (*www.gnu.org/*): UNIX database package.
   WebLint (*www.weblint.org/*): Check for defunct links to other sites.
   Bobby (*www.cast.org/bobby/*): Web page accessibility tool.
   WebTrends (*www.webtrends.com/*): Analyze server logs.
   Netscape Composer (*www.netscape.com/*): Remote WWW publishing.

NOTES

1. MadSci policy for handling questions is found at: *www.madsci.org/info/using.html*
2. Documentation on the Common Gateway Interface may be found at: *http://hoohoo.ncsa.uiuc.edu/cgi/*

3. Invariably, some unquantified number of these users did not intend to ask a question, and so may not have proceeded to ask one if given immediate access to the question form. In addition, users who jumped to our search engine or other resources on our site may have returned eventually to ask a question beyond the one hour latent period defined to indicate unique sessions for a given Internet address.

4. User "sessions" were followed over a two-month period in 1997 by analyzing the paths of users in the server logs.

Digital Reference Service at the Georgia Institute of Technology

Bruce Henson

Georgia Tech's digital reference service was five years old in October 1999. Its components currently include ASK a Librarian (ASK), an e-mail and Web reference service, and Real Time Reference, an online reference service using chat software. ASK a Librarian was created in 1994 and has proven a success due to its consistency, quality of service, and availability. Real Time Reference was implemented in May 1999.

CREATION OF ASK A LIBRARIAN

The idea to develop the ASK a Librarian service was the result of reference discussion groups at the 1994 ALA Annual Conference. ASK a Librarian was available for the library's October InfoFair, a week-long open house, and the first question was received on October 9, 1994 (Johnston and Grusin, 1995). ASK was coordinated by Pat Johnston, Reference Librarian, until 1998 and was initially staffed by three reference librarians and one library assistant. The staff checked the service twice daily for messages and provided responses within one workday.

From the beginning, ASK was included on the opening menu of the Georgia Tech Electronic Library (GTEL) (*www.library.gatech.edu*); this system contains the library catalog and locally mounted and remote databases. Placement on this easily accessible menu has likely contributed to the success of ASK. As the library migrated to a Web-based system, ASK remained on the GTEL opening page and is also on the standard button bar available throughout GTEL.

ASK is restricted by GTEL password to the Georgia Tech community of students, faculty, and staff. Use of the password automatically identifies the client and enables the system to place the client name and e-mail address on each request. The ASK form also asks clients for the best way to get in touch with them (e.g., e-mail, phone, or fax) and has a text box for the client's question. The service occasionally receives questions from individuals outside of Georgia Tech via the library's systems department. Any Institute-related messages received by the systems department are forwarded to ASK.

ASK A LIBRARIAN TODAY

The ASK a Librarian service is currently staffed by six librarians and three library assistants who check twice daily for messages and respond within one workday. The staff base has expanded to include library staff outside of the reference department, including (on a periodic basis) the head of technical resources, the head of acquisitions, and assistant director for access services. Service has proven to be a fertile training ground for new reference department staff, who work alongside experienced ASK staff. The luxury of having the unpressured time to refer to colleagues and locate information is an advantage for both new and veteran employees.

The service was updated in 1998 from a text-based e-mail system to a graphical user interface (GUI) environment. Accompanying the change was: a new staffing schedule, a system of archiving transactions electronically rather than in paper, the addition of a brief client information form, the creation of an online user manual, implementing an ongoing assessment survey, and expanded service hours from five to six days per week. The new staffing schedule includes both a primary person and a backup person who are responsible for the service each day; the backup person assists the primary person if the question volume is high and assumes primary responsibility when the primary person is absent. The client information form includes a question about the client's status (e.g., faculty, staff, undergraduate or graduate student), in addition to the question regarding the best way to contact the client. In spring 1999, an assessment survey was constructed and mounted on the Web using the *AskA Starter Kit* (Lankes and Kasowitz, 1998) as a guide, and is currently used in an ongoing monthly survey of ASK clients.

STATISTICS AND ASSESSMENT

Georgia Tech Library Reference Statistics from 1994–99 are very revealing. They show that 297 questions were received within the first nine months of the ASK service (October 1994–June 1995), indicating that 1994 was an opportune time to implement electronic reference at Georgia Tech. During its first two full fiscal years, the number of questions rose dramatically to 686 in 1995–96 and dropped slightly to 650 during 1996–97. Interestingly, the number of ASK questions declined by approximately 19 percent during 1997–98 and 1998–99, with 526 and 546 queries respectively. Conjectures for this decline are that an increasing number of clients are electronically sophisticated and adept at navigating the electronic library, and that some clients simply bypass the library and find their resources on the Web, regardless of quality.

A comparison of user statistics from April 1995 and June 1999 shows that the percentage of graduate students using ASK has increased from 41 percent to 48 percent, while undergraduate use has decreased from 35 percent to 26 percent, and faculty use has decreased from 24 percent to 13 percent. In an April 1995 survey, ASK clients rated their satisfaction with the service as follows: 52 percent excellent, 33 percent good, 5 percent adequate, and 10 percent not satisfied (Johnston and Grusin, 1995: 48). In a June 1999 survey[1], ASK clients rated the usefulness and effectiveness of the service on a scale of 1 to 5 (1 is the highest ranking). Eighty-four percent chose 1 or 2, indicating that the service was considered very useful and effective by most respondents. Other 1999 survey questions show that 39 percent of respondents used ASK more than once; 91 percent received a response within the promised time of one workday; 94 percent received a response that was presented in a clear and understandable way; and 94 percent of the responses provided an answer or led to an answer for the client's question.

NEW INITIATIVES FOR ASK A LIBRARIAN

We are in the process of implementing a client form for ASK that will more closely approximate an in-person reference interview. Use of the form will hopefully eliminate the "high dialog penalties" of multiple e-mail messages, prevent the elimination of critical information from the client, and forestall assumptions made by ASK staff (Sloan, 1998b). The form will also standardize the electronic reference interview, which seems to be more critical than the in-person reference interview. Bernie Sloan (1998a) states the formats of in-person and e-mail reference "are more complementary than duplicative" (p. 80). In a study comparing characteristics of e-mail, in-person, and telephone reference interviews, Eileen Abels (1996) confirms Sloan's belief. Abels' study shows that e-mail interviews are remote, noninteractive, nonverbal, and use written language, in-person interviews are interactive and use both verbal and nonverbal language, and telephone interviews are remote, interactive, and use verbal language. Abels' study of e-mail reference interviews at the University of Maryland identifies five types of reference interviews: piecemeal, feedback, bombardment, assumption, and systematic. The systematic reference interview method, which includes the use of a client form, proved to be the most efficient in regard to successful results and reduced number of e-mail interactions between the client and the responder.

ASK a Librarian traditionally has offered assistance with "brief reference questions." We are assessing now whether that limiting phrase discourages the use of the service by distance. It seems likely, however, that our level of digital reference service should expand as our digital library resources and their users have increased. Digital reference services are value-added services, which will not replace traditional reference transactions. A library's goal, however, must be to design services that consider its clients' needs and the institution's mission statement, balanced with time and budget restraints. The library increasingly loses its identity to its remote users. The effects of increased remote use of the library are discussed in the literature. Anne Lipow (1998: 47) states unequivocally, "it is not the user who is becoming remote from the library; it is the library that is becoming remote from the user." Increasingly, Ann Wolpert writes (1998: 33), the "brand identity . . . that resides in a high quality on-campus library" is lost to remote clients, as interactions and communication with library staff decrease or are nonexistent. Bernie Sloan notes (1998b: 119), a majority of definitions of, and discussions about digital libraries have "an emphasis on technology and information resources and a very noticeable lack of discussion of the service aspects."

It generally takes longer to answer a digital reference question than an in-person question, and there may be transitions and tradeoffs for librarians if we expand our policy to include in-depth research assistance to our digital clients. To fulfill our mission and retain our identity, however, in-depth reference service may need to be included digitally, so that the same level of quality service is available for all library clients.

Most libraries host client bases that are comprised mostly of local users, as indicated by results of digital reference surveys from other libraries (Bushwallow-Wilbur, DeVinney, and Whitcomb, 1996). In keeping with this trend, ASK a Librarian's largest client base is located physically in the Atlanta Metropolitan area, mostly on campus. We are in the process of marketing our digital reference services to Georgia Tech's undergraduate students, rapidly growing distance education population, and large number of international students (who are frequently more comfortable communicating in English through writing rather than speaking). Although digital reference service is used infrequently by distance education clients, these students have similar needs to local remote users and seem to be a promising potential client base.

REAL TIME REFERENCE

The idea for Georgia Tech's Real Time Reference service evolved out of discussions at the 1999 ALA Midwinter meeting. The Real Time Reference service uses America Online's Instant Messenger chat feature to enable clients to ask and receive answers to questions online. The service is installed currently on a reference desk PC and is available the entire time the Reference Desk is staffed; a bell indicates incoming messages. Real Time was offered initially during limited hours with staff monitoring the service from their desks; staff members found it too constricting to be restricted to their desks during the hours of service. By moving the service to the reference desk area and having responsibility for the service assigned to staff covering the reference desk, the service was expanded from 15 hours to 87 hours per week. Real Time has not proven to be as instantly popular as ASK. However, the service has had 22 clients since its implementation in May 1999. Currently we are investigating other software options for the service that would not require that clients download software and would enable us to archive transactions.

CONCLUSION

The Georgia Institute of Technology Library has striven to design services from a client perspective, with the Institute's mission statement in mind. Its digital reference service has clearly served a client need the past five years. As the volume of digital resources and remote clients rapidly grow, it is imperative that the library offer human interaction where and when we are able. To fulfill our mission, retain our "brand identity," and maximize our potential client base, the Tech Library is expanding its digital reference services to remote clients. As the library has become less of a physical place and more of a function, it is imperative that our reference services are available to our clients.

NOTES

1. The following statistics are from responses to the 1999 survey conducted by the Georgia Institute of Technology Library Reference Department.

REFERENCES

Abels, Eileen G. 1996. "The E-mail Reference Interview." *RQ* 35 (Spring): 347.
Bushwallow-Wilbur, Lara, Gemma DeVinney, and Fritz Whitcomb. 1996. "Electronic Mail Reference Service: A Study." *RQ* 35, no. 3 (Spring): 359–63.

Johnston, Pat and Ann Grusin. 1995. "Personal Service in an Impersonal World: Throwing Life Preservers to Those Drowning in an Ocean of Information." *The Georgia Librarian* 32: 45–49.

Lankes, R. David and Abby S. Kasowitz. 1998. *AskA Starter Kit: How to Build and Maintain Digital Reference Services*. Syracuse, N.Y.: ERIC Clearinghouse on Information & Technology.

Lipow, Anne Grodzins. 1998. "Reference Services in a Digital Age." *Reference & User Services Quarterly* 38, no. 1 (Fall): 47.

Sloan, Bernie. 1998a. "Electronic Reference Services: Some Suggested Guidelines." *Reference & User Services Quarterly* 38, no. 1 (Fall): 80.

Sloan, Bernie. 1998b. "Service Perspectives for the Digital Library." *Library Trends* 47 (Summer): 117–43.

Wolpert, Ann. 1998. "Services to Remote Users: Marketing the Library's Role." *Library Trends* 47 (Summer): 33.

Part IV

Evaluating Digital
Reference Services

OVERVIEW

The field of digital reference introduces new aspects of reference service evaluation. While some assessment methods and experiences are similar to those of traditional reference, digital reference presents new issues in terms of identifying response quality, user expectations and satisfaction, applications of research methods, and target audiences. Although some digital reference services and consortia have begun to establish quality criteria (see Part 3), there have been very few studies to determine quality and effectiveness of individual services.

This section describes two different digital reference services—one from an academic library and one from a national museum library. The authors discuss methods for assessing each service and results of recently conducted research studies. The two papers in this section provide helpful information to researchers as well as other digital reference services interested in evaluating aspects of service. Both make a valuable contribution to the literature on digital reference evaluation and hopefully pave the way for future studies.

Evaluating the "Ask a Question" Service at the University of California, Irvine

Judy Horn and Kathryn Kjaer

This paper examines the three methods used by the University of California, Irvine Libraries to evaluate its electronic reference service: statistical analysis, user surveys, and quality review. Such an evaluation allowed the service to better meet the needs of its users and to suggest recommendations for improvements in the future, such as implementing a software package that can analyze statistics and track questions and answers, and adding a chat feature to allow for a reference interview with those users whose questions are unclear. Appendices include guidelines developed to ensure that a consistent level of service is provided, templates for responses to frequently asked questions, and user surveys.

BACKGROUND

Recognizing that electronic reference is rapidly becoming an established part of reference service in academic libraries, the University of California, Irvine (UCI) Libraries established an electronic reference service team in August 1998 with the goal of beginning its "Ask a Question" service on September 15, 1998. This date coincided with the debut of a new redesigned UCI Libraries Web page. The electronic reference service team achieved this goal and the first electronic reference question was received from a medical student on September 21. During the first month, "Ask a Question" could be found only at the second and third levels of the Website. We quickly recognized that if people were to use it, the service needed to be displayed prominently on the front page. When we moved an announcement of the "Ask a Question" service to the first page, the number of questions received immediately increased. The "Ask a Question" entry on the first page links users directly to a series of boxes where they can ask their question and also read the service policies.

The policies and procedures for the "Ask a Question" service were established by the electronic reference service team, which is composed of two librarians and a library assistant from the science library and two librarians and a library assistant from the main library. The first year was designated as a pilot phase. The team established the following policies:

- Questions, except those received on weekends and holidays, are answered within 24 hours.
- The targeted audience for the service is UCI faculty, students, and staff. We will answer questions from nonaffiliated persons if they involve UCI or its resources.
- Suggested alternatives are provided for nonaffiliated persons when we are unable to answer the question.
- Types of questions that will be answered include requests for brief factual or statistical information, questions about which resources to use, and questions about the UCI Libraries' resources, services, and facilities.

Questions received by "Ask a Question" are answered by the members of the electronic reference service team. Each member of the team is assigned a day to answer the questions in the inbox. On difficult questions, team members consult among each other or contact a knowledgeable source. Questions are not referred to others to answer except in rare instances. This puts each team member in a situation similar to that of being on a general reference desk in which the person on the desk at that time must address any question asked. There are obvious pros and cons to this method of sharing the questions, but with team members' backgrounds in science, social sciences, humanities, and government information, it is working quite efficiently and effectively.

The team developed guidelines to assure that a consistent level of service is provided. The first five items in the guidelines are included below. The complete list of guidelines is included as Appendix A.

1. The team member responsible for answering questions should check the inbox of "Ask a Question" frequently throughout the day that they are assigned and respond promptly to all questions.
2. If team members will be unavailable on days assigned to them (on vacation, ill, etc.), they are responsible for arranging for a replacement.
3. Questions from non-UCI users:
   a. If the question pertains to resources or services of the UCI Libraries or the UCI campus, try to answer completely.
   b. If the question is a general reference question that does not relate specifically to the UCI Libraries or the UCI campus, reply using the template "NON-UCI IN-DEPTH REFERENCE REQUEST." Occasionally, it may be appropriate for a team member to provide the answer to a general reference question, especially when the information readily is available and does not require in-depth research.
4. Try to provide answers to specific questions, but also include an explanation of how to find the information.
5. Always cite the source in which you find the answer to the question. This could be a Web page, a reference book, a database, etc.

Additionally, the team developed templates for responses to frequently asked questions (FAQ). Templates were developed for such FAQs as in-depth subject reference requests from non-UCI affiliated users, information on how to renew a book online, and requests that the library purchase certain books or electronic resources (see Appendix B).

The service has grown slowly and receives an average of about 55 questions per month. In addition to moving "Ask a Question" to the front page of the libraries' Web page, "Ask a Question" was featured in a quarterly library newsletter for faculty. The service was also advertised on bookmarks, by librarians at bibliographic instruction sessions, and at meetings with public services library staff.

EVALUATION OF ELECTRONIC REFERENCE SERVICE

The main purpose of an evaluation of an electronic reference service is to assure that the goals and objectives of the service are being met and to ascertain that the service is working efficiently and effectively. The methods for evaluating electronic reference service are similar to those used for traditional reference service with a slightly different focus. The focus in electronic reference service is the quality of the response, user satisfaction with the response, and the question-answer process that has been established (Lankes and Kasowitz, 1998). While there are many methods for evaluating such a service, among the most useful are statistical analysis, user survey, and quality review. These three methods have been used at the University of California, Irvine to evaluate its "Ask a Question" service.

STATISTICAL ANALYSIS

The University of California, Irvine collected data on the number of questions asked, the affiliation of the user, the type of questions, the day of the week and the time the question was asked. Statistical analysis of this information provides valuable data that assist in improving the process and the efficiency of the service. Statistical analysis can also provide a benchmark to measure goals and objectives. Additionally, statistical analysis can assist in determining the appropriate level and subject expertise of those who answer the questions, staffing patterns, and whether service is reaching the target audience, and can assist in justifying the benefits of the service to decision makers.

Types of Users and Questions

In addition to statistics on the number of users, UCI has compiled statistics on the status and affiliation of the users. These statistics have been used to determine whether we are reaching our target audience, which includes the UCI faculty, students, and staff. Service statistics show that 53 percent of the questions received come from UCI faculty, students and staff, indicating that the service is receiving the bulk of its questions from its target audience. Statistics on the type of questions asked indicate that 76 percent of the questions are reference questions and 17 percent are categorized as access questions (e.g., how to check out a book, how to renew books, how to get a Personal Identification Number). Access questions are most frequently asked by undergraduate students (31 percent), followed by graduate students (24 percent). Non-UCI affiliated users are most likely to ask questions about library holdings (56 percent).

Another statistic that we have found useful is the type of questions received from non-UCI affiliated people. Although we have received questions from several states and at least 12 foreign countries, including England, Scotland, Belgium, Netherlands, Japan, India, Korea, Hong Kong, Mexico, South Africa, Saudia Arabia, and Brazil, it is interesting to note that 61 percent of the questions from non-UCI affiliated users are on subjects involving the collections and services of the UCI Libraries or the UCI campus, as opposed to general reference topics.

Days and Times of Activity

The day of the week or the time of the day that most questions are asked is important to consider in determining staffing and provides valuable data for planning an interactive service. According to the data, the three most popular days for questions are Wednesday, Tuesday, and Monday, in that order, and the last popular day is Saturday. The three most popular times for questions were 10 A.M–12 noon; 12 noon–2 P.M. and 2–4 P.M., coinciding with the busiest times at the reference desk. This was surprising, because it was expected that most of the questions would be sent while the reference desk was closed.

Turnaround Time

Since users are promised a response to their questions within 24 hours (except for weekends and holidays), it was necessary to determine whether this objective has been met. Statistics show that the average length of time between the question and the answer is seven hours. The longest time between a question and answer was 22.5 hours and the shortest time during a weekday was four minutes. These statistics indicate that the goal is being achieved but they also indicate that the service should consider and implement ways of answering the questions more quickly.

USER SURVEYS

UCI also conducted surveys to evaluate "Ask a Question." These surveys provide the opportunity to find out about the service from the user's perspective. The design of the survey affects the type of information that is ultimately acquired. Three user surveys were conducted to obtain data on "Ask a Question." Two of these surveys were conducted by the electronic reference service team and the third was part of an Instructional Technology Faculty Survey that was sponsored jointly by the Office of Academic Computing, the UCI Libraries, and the Division of Undergraduate Education.

The first user survey was conducted in June 1999. E-mail surveys were sent to UCI faculty, students, and staff who had asked a question during the month of May. The survey was sent to UCI-affiliated users only because they represent the target group and their questions were answered without referral to another source (which may not have been the case with questions from non-UCI affiliated users). This survey asked five questions and used the ranking analysis with a scale of 1–5 with 5 being the highest (see Appendix C). Twenty-eight surveys were sent and thirteen responses were received, nine of which ranked the service at its highest levels (4–5). The other two responses ranked the service at the 3 and 2 levels. All respondents indicated they would use the service again. One responder who rated the service lower did so because he or she had expected an instantaneous response (in spite of the statement about 24 hours in our service policy). This person received a response within 30 minutes of the question, but was still dissatisfied with the timeliness of the response.

The second survey was the Instructional Technology Faculty Survey that was conducted in the spring of 1999. One question on the survey asked faculty if they currently used, had ever used, or planned to use "Ask a Question". Only about 8 percent of the faculty indicated that they were using or had used the service. This number matches our statistics of the percentage of faculty users. As a result of this low number, the team discussed ways to publicize the service more to faculty and whether the position of the "Ask a Question" link on the front page of the UCI Libraries Website really was visible to our users.

This led the team to develop another user survey of UCI faculty, students, and staff who asked questions during the months of July and August (see Appendix D). Forty-four e-mail surveys were sent and 19 responses were received. This survey asked users how they found out about the service. This time, the questions were framed to facilitate a qualitative analysis. This was done by giving the user multiple choices for each question. For instance, possible responses to the question, "How would you rate the quality of the response to your question?" ranged from "It was all of the information that I needed" to "It was not helpful at all." Users were asked to rate the quality of the service, the response time, and their overall satisfaction with the service. Sixteen of the 19 respondents found out about the service through the "Ask a Question" link on the UCI Libraries Web page; this indicated that our link is indeed in a visible place and is being utilized. On the quality of the response, 16 respondents indicated they received "all the information needed" and four indicated that it was "helpful but not complete." All 19 respondents said that the response was returned quickly and in time to meet their needs. Regarding their overall satisfaction with the service, 16 were "very satisfied" and three were "somewhat satisfied." All said that they would use the service again. Following each of the questions, the user was asked to provide comments. This user survey was more useful and provided more substantive information than the first one. The multiple choice questions and the opportunity to respond provided a better sense of the users' needs and satisfaction than the ranking analysis.

QUALITY REVIEW

Evaluating the quality of the responses to questions is another very important component of electronic reference service. With electronic reference service, even more so than on a reference desk, the response to an electronic reference question becomes the "main product of the service" (Lankes and Kasowitz, 1998: 185). It is important that the quality of the responses be evaluated in some way. Lankes and Kasowitz (1998) suggest several methods of measuring staff performance including user surveys, unobtrusive testing, peer assessment, grading or tracking, and self-assessment. At UCI only professional librarians respond to electronic reference questions. It is difficult to determine a good objective means of evaluating the quality of an answer. Frequently, the perception of quality or lack of quality is based on the reviewer's expertise in that subject or on the interpretation of the question. One of the most effective methods that the UCI team has found of reviewing the quality of responses is to discuss each response as a group. This provides an opportunity for the expert in that area to make suggestions for future responses as well as for others to ask questions or suggest ways to improve the quality of the answer. The sessions are not critical but rather mentoring sessions with questions like "Did you consider . . . ?," "There is a new source that you might not know about," or "Next time you might want to consider this." When regular meetings are not possible, the members of the team really miss this interaction since it is a very effective learning method for all team members. This type of team assessment has played a very important role in assuring the quality of responses, and it has worked well in the professional environment.

CONCLUSION

This first year of "Ask a Question" has been a valuable learning experience. The team has submitted a report (*http:// sun3.lib.uci.edu/~question*) containing detailed statistics, and a flowchart as well as the guidelines, templates, and user surveys included in this paper. The team recommends that "Ask a Question" be established as a permanent service for the library and that time spent by librarians on "Ask a Question" be counted as part of their reference service workload. Currently, answering "Ask a Question" queries is an additional task for librarians on the team.

The report makes several project recommendations for the team for next year. One of the major issues is that the current software is not conducive to tracking and preparing statistical analysis of the questions. The team is now using the libraries' e-mail software (Pine) and has had to make various adjustments in order to perform certain functions. Unfortunately, all of the statistical analysis had to be done manually. One goal is to implement a software package that can provide the team with the necessary statistics as well as track the questions and answers.

We have learned the value of regular systematic evaluation and of quality review of responses. A major goal is to resume weekly meetings (which were cancelled during the summer) at which responses from questions received the previous week will be the focus of discussion.

One of the shortcomings of this type of electronic reference service is its lack of immediate interactivity. Questions are often unclear and there is no way to do a reference interview. Given this, and the assumptions of instantaneous service by some users, the team will discuss how to add a chat or MOO (MUD, Object-Oriented) feature to the service. Statistics regarding the busiest days and hours of service will be reviewed during these discussions.

It is anticipated that the use of this service will steadily increase. One faculty member described it in the Instructional Technology Faculty Survey as "a godsend." The information acquired in the various evaluations have provided the team with concrete and valuable data that will assist them in implementing improvements in staffing, scheduling, quality and timeliness of responses, as well as in offering direction for the future of the "Ask a Question" service.

APPENDIX A

Guidelines for Ask A Question Responses

1. The team member responsible for answering questions should check the e-mail inbox of "Ask a Question" frequently throughout the day they are assigned and respond promptly to all questions.
2. If team members will be unavailable on their assigned day (on vacation, ill, etc.), they are responsible to arrange for a replacement.
3. Questions from non-UCI users:
   a. If the question pertains to resources or services of the UCI Libraries or the UCI campus, try to answer completely.
   b. If the question is a general reference question that does not relate specifically to the UCI Libraries or the UCI campus, reply using the template "NON-UCI IN-DEPTH REFERENCE REQUEST."
   c. Occasionally, it may be appropriate for a team member to provide the answer to a general reference question, especially when the information is available and does not require in-depth research.
4. Try to provide answers to specific questions, but also include an explanation of how to find the information.
5. Always cite the source in which you find the answer to the question. This could be a Web page, a reference book, a database, etc.
6. Never simply forward a question to another library staff member. If you need to consult with other library staff (ERS team member, loan desk, interlibrary loan, or bibliographer, etc.) in order to provide a complete answer, you may send a brief response to the user explaining you are working on the question and will get back soon.
7. Referrals: When you receive a question that could be answered more accurately or completely by another librarian, another office on campus, or a non-UCI agency or library, etc., send an immediate response to the user with

the name and contact information (e-mail, phone, URL, etc.).

8. Use judgment when responding to UCI student questions. If it seems the student is asking you for the specific answer to a homework question, try to instruct the student on how to find the answer rather than doing the research for the student.

9. Use judgment when responding to faculty or staff questions. While it can be very helpful to explain how to find the information, try to provide the specific answers to questions if possible.

10. When a question from a UCI student, faculty, or staff member requires more in-depth assistance than allowed by the guidelines listed on the "Ask a Question" Service electronic form (*www.lib.uci.edu/serv/ask.html*), suggest the user come into the library for personal assistance or refer the user to a subject specialist as appropriate.

11. Collection development questions and suggestions should be referred to the appropriate bibliographer. Use the template "COLLECTION DEVELOPMENT REFERRAL." Examples: "Why don't we subscribe to this electronic journal?" "Can the library buy this book?"

12. Comments, complaints, and suggestions about library services, facilities, or staff should be referred to the manager of the appropriate library unit. Be sure to respond immediately to the user indicating that you have referred the comment to the appropriate person.

13. Replies concerning the "Ask a Question Service," both positive and negative, should be forwarded to all members of the team and saved in the "questions" folder.

APPENDIX B

Templates for Responses to Frequently Asked Questions

Non-UCI In-depth Reference Request

Response to non-UCI user requesting non-UCI specific information/research assistance:

Dear _____,

We are sorry, but the UCI Libraries "Ask a Question" service is not able to provide in-depth research assistance to individuals who are not UCI students, faculty, or staff.

We suggest you try the Internet Public Library at: *www.ipl.org/ref/QUE/* , or Ask an Expert (*www.askanexpert.com/askanexpert/index.html*) for e-mail help with your question. Otherwise, you may come in to one of our libraries (*www.lib.uci.edu/about.html*) where reference librarians can show you resources and help with your research. Of course, don't forget your local school or public library. They may have just the resources you need.

—"Ask a Question" Team

Collection Development Referral

Response to patron who wants the library to purchase a book, journal, etc., or to license an electronic journal or electronic resource:

Dear _____,

We are forwarding your question to _____, who is the UCI Libraries Subject Librarian/Bibliographer for_____.

Whenever you would like to suggest a title (online or print) be added to the UCI Libraries collection, please address your request to the appropriate subject librarian/bibliographer. A list of subject librarians and contact information is available at: *www.lib.uci.edu/about/sublib.html*.

—"Ask a Question" Team

Renew a Book

Response to "How do I renew a book online?":

Dear _____,

You may renew your books online through the ANTPAC online catalog.

From the ANTPAC home page (*antpac.lib.uci.edu/*) select "View your circulation record" from the buttons on the left.

On the information page that follows, select "View your circulation record" again.

On the next page, you will need to enter your name, your library barcode number, and your Personal Identification Number, or PIN. If you do not already have a PIN, you must come to one of the library loan desks and get one from a loan desk assistant.

On the next screen, you should see your name, address, and phone number displayed. Click on the button indicating the number of items you have currently checked out.

On the next screen, you may select to renew all items, or you may select the specific titles you want to renew. A new due date will appear under status. Or you may see a message that it is not possible to renew the book at this time.

If you have any further questions about renewing your books, we suggest you call one of the Loan Desks for further information:

Main Library: (949) 824–6842
Science Library: (949) 824–3692
Medical Center Library: (714) 456–5583

—"Ask a Question" Team

APPENDIX C

User Survey #1

(E-mailed to UCI affiliated users of "Ask a Question" during May, 1999)

Dear Ask a Question user:

During the month of May, you sent a question either to the UCI Libraries "Ask a Question" service or to the Comments box on the Libraries' homepage and received an answer from "Ask a Question."

To assist us in making improvements in this service, we would like some feedback from you and would appreciate it if you would take just a few minutes to answer the questions below.

Participation in this survey is voluntary and all information will be kept anonymous and confidential. Your name will not be used in any way, and no one will know about your specific answers except the "Ask a Question" staff.

Please forward your response to *libraries@uci.edu*.

Thank you for your time and cooperation.

—"Ask a Question" Team

University of California
The UCI Libraries
P.O. Box 19557
Irvine, CA 92623-9557
www.lib.uci.edu/serv/ask.html

Ask a Question Survey

1. Are you UCI_____faculty_____staff_____graduate student_____undergraduate?
2. Please rate the following on a scale of 1–5 (with 5 being the highest)
   ___How well did the response answer your question or lead you to the answer?
   ___How well did the time between the submission of your question and the answer meet your needs?

___How would you rate your overall satisfaction with the service?

3. Would you use the service again? YES___NO___
4. Why did you choose to use "Ask a Question"?

APPENDIX D

User Survey #2

(E-mailed to UCI affiliated users of "Ask a Question" during July–August, 1999)

Dear Ask a Question user:

During the month of July or August, you sent a question either to the UCI Libraries' "Ask a Question" service or to the Comments box on the Libraries' homepage and received an answer from "Ask a Question."

To assist us in making improvements in this service, we would like some feedback from you and would appreciate it if you would take just a few minutes to answer the questions below.

Participation in this survey is voluntary and all information will be kept anonymous and confidential. Your name will not be used in any way, and no one will know about your specific answers except the "Ask a Question" staff.

Please forward your response to *libraries@uci.edu*.

Thank you for your time and cooperation.

—"Ask a Question" Team

University of California
The UCI Libraries
P.O. Box 19557
Irvine, CA 92623–9557
www.lib.uci.edu/serv/ask.html

Ask a Question Survey

1. What is your affiliation with UCI?
   ____ Faculty
   ____ Staff
   ____ Graduate Student
   ____ Undergraduate

2. How did you find out about this service?

____ I found the Ask a Question link on the UCI Libraries homepage (*www.lib.uci.edu/*)

____ I was referred to the service by a librarian

____ I heard about it in a library instruction class

____ I heard about it from a teacher

____ Other. Please explain:

3. Why did you choose to use the "Ask a Question" Service?

4. How would you rate the quality of the response to your question?

____ It was all the information I needed

____ It was helpful, but not complete

____ It was not helpful at all

Why?

5. How would you rate the response time (time between the submission of your question and the receipt of the answer)?

____ Response came quickly and in time to meet my needs

____ Response was slower than I expected, but came in time to meet my needs

____ Response took too long and not in time to meet my needs

Why?

6. How would you rate your overall satisfaction with the "Ask a Question" service?

____ Very satisfied

____ Somewhat satisfied

____ Not at all satisfied

Why?

7. Would you use this service again?

____ Yes

____ No

Why?

8. Do you have any suggestions or comments on how we might improve the service?

REFERENCES

Lankes, R. David and Abby S. Kasowitz. 1988. *The AskA Starter Kit: How to Build and Maintain Digital Reference Services*. Syracuse, N.Y.: ERIC Clearinghouse on Information & Technology.

National Museum of American Art Reference Desk: A Usage Analysis of a Digital Reference Service

Laura Sowers and Marilyn Domas White

This paper presents partial findings of a multi-part study characterizing the use of the digital reference service offered by the National Museum of American Art (NMAA) and assessing its effectiveness in meeting the information needs of its clients. The study is based on a survey of a sample of clients submitting questions to NMAA's reference desk between June 1997 and May 1998 and an analysis of their questions and responses. This paper presents the findings of the survey, which looks at the following research questions: (1) What are the characteristics of the clients of the NMAA digital reference service?, (2) What is the level of use of the service?, (3) What are the possible explanations?, (4) What is the nature of the response?, and (5) How effective is the digital reference service, based on client assessments of the response? The relevant population consisted of individuals who had submitted questions between June 1997 and May 1998. The user study, one of the few that have been done by outside researchers for an electronic question/answer service in a nonacademic library, raises interesting questions about methodologies for user studies of virtual audiences and users' expectations in the electronic environment.

The widespread popularity and growth in the use of the Internet and e-mail have facilitated the extension of library services into this electronic arena. Digital reference services, in particular, offer the public access to traditional library services in an online environment. These services may operate from libraries or other institutions with information resources useful to the public. Often called Ask an Expert or AskA services, they link the public with experts in a particular field.

The body of literature on digital reference is growing but tends to focus on the development and structure of the services rather than on clients' usage and expectations of digital reference. Most research also concentrates on digital reference services in academic settings.

Fishman (1998) outlines issues and problems to be considered during the planning of a digital reference service. Using the service at the University of Maryland at Baltimore's Health Sciences Library as an example, she describes the question load a service might encounter and illustrates the benefits and advantages of digital reference over traditional forms of reference service. Still and Campbell (1993) describe early digital reference systems at several universities and their evolution with changing technology. Ryan (1996) also discusses the development of digital reference services and then studies in detail the Internet Public Library's reference services. Her case study of the IPL sheds light on the types of questions a digital reference service encounters and the challenges staff face in responding effectively and efficiently.

Other studies on the design and implementation of digital reference services include Lankes' (1998) examination of several services' question-answering processes. White (1999) developed a framework for analyzing and evaluating digital reference services, which has been applied to 11 different services. The e-mail reference interview receives close attention in Abels (1996) and Tibbo (1995). Hahn's (1997) study of a university computer help desk investigates both staff and users' expectations and satisfaction with question negotiation via e-mail.

This study investigates the use of one particular digital reference service, the National Museum of American Art (NMAA) Reference Desk.[1]

NMAA REFERENCE DESK

The National Museum of American Art's digital reference service, which appeared on America Online in 1993, was among the first services intended to answer questions from a national audience. As the Internet became more accessible through the World Wide Web, the service moved to NMAA's new Website. Currently it is located under "Study Center" (*nmaa-ryder.si.edu/study/index.html*). Drawing on NMAA's extensive resources, the service answers questions about American art from clients at all levels of education and from all areas of the United States and many foreign countries (Stahl 1998a; Stahl 1998b).

Like many AskA services, the NMAA digital reference service's Website provides a form that requests information from clients about themselves and their question, including level of education, sources already checked, and the time in which a response is expected. The form encourages clients to be as specific as possible about their questions, aiding librarians in providing patrons with "brief, usable, and convenient information communicated in a personalized manner" (Stahl 1998a, 68). During the time period studied, questions were answered by one librarian with the occasional help of interns or other staff. Staffing resources have increased since then, and now two librarians and library science interns assist in responding to questions.

RESEARCH QUESTIONS

This study seeks to characterize the use of the digital reference service offered by NMAA and assess its effectiveness in meeting the information needs of its clients. Specific research questions include:

1. What are the characteristics of the clients of the NMAA digital reference service?
2. What is the level of use of the service?
3. What are the possible explanations?
4. What is the nature of the response?

5. How effective is the digital reference service, based on client assessments of response?

The relevant population consisted of individuals who had submitted questions between June 1997 and May 1998.

METHODOLOGY

Sample

From June 1997 to May 1998, the NMAA service received 3,968 messages. Although the unit of analysis in this survey is the individual submitting the question, the archives could not be sorted easily to identify all clients. The archive was arranged by day, with messages generally ordered according to time submitted. As a result, a 10 percent sample of messages was drawn by days (i.e., all messages on a particular day in the sample were included). The initial sample of 383 constituted a 9.7 percent sample of the total number of messages received during this time, representing 383 different clients. Subsequently, this sample was modified to omit children (28, 7 percent), as noted in the grade level information on the query form plus a few responses, resulting in an adjusted sample of 355 clients aged 18 and over.

Data-Gathering

For this paper, the data were gathered through an e-mail survey. For other parts of this study, additional data-gathering techniques were used. The questionnaire used the critical incident technique. Respondents answered the questions based on particular queries they had submitted. The original submission and response were included with the questionnaire. Since the service had originally responded to the client in one of three ways (response with answer; response soliciting additional information; no response), three variants of the questionnaire were used with slight modifications based on the differences in the service's response. Appendix A includes the cover letter and Appendix B includes the questionnaire, with all three variants noted.

Response Rate

Of the adjusted sample of 355 clients, 80 (23 percent) of the questionnaires were returned because of problems with addresses, resulting in 275 questionnaires transmitted successfully. From this adjusted sample, 66 questionnaires were returned (24 percent). Of these, 53 (80 percent of returns, 19 percent of adjusted *N* of questionnaires) were complete and useful; an additional 13 (20 percent of returns, 5 percent of adjusted *N* of questionnaires) were returned without answering the questions but with general comments about the service. These percentages are based on an initial mailing, followed by a second mailing two weeks later. Possible reasons for the low response rate were client difficulties in interacting with the e-mail survey form; perceived length of the questionnaire because it was accompanied by the original question and response; the length of time between submitting the question and the survey; and the lack of attachment and sense of duty to a service where human contact is relatively minimal. The low response rate limits the generalizability of the findings, but they are presented here since so little is known about client behavior in connection with digital reference services.[2]

Respondent Characteristics

Most of the respondents (44, 83 percent) had used the NMAA Reference Desk only one time during the year in question. The remaining 12 (17 percent) were repeat clients. With the exception of one person who had used the service 10 times during the year, the repeat clients had used the service an average of 2.6 times per year (standard deviation 1.06). Approximately 64 percent of the respondents were female, 36 percent male.

ANALYSIS AND RESULTS

Geographic Location of Clients and Time of Query

Do digital reference services attract new clients or do they essentially offer a more convenient form of the service to the same client? These questions can be addressed by looking at the geographic locations of the clients and the times when they submit questions. The clients of this service were located in 28 states and three foreign countries (Canada, Israel, and Italy), which indicates that NMAA, which is physically located in Washington, D.C., is reaching beyond its immediate geographic location for clients with this digital reference service. NMAA has a national mission:

> The National Museum of American Art is the nation's museum dedicated to the arts and artists of the United States from earliest colonial times to the present day. As a federal institution, the museum serves audiences throughout the land, as well as those who visit its two historic landmark buildings in Washington, D.C. The museum presents for a broad public its collections, educational materials, and research resources, which reflect the diversity of the country's citizenry (U.S. National Museum of American Art, 1998).

Occasionally respondents referred to difficulties posed by their own geographic locations. A reader in Nebraska commented, "Our research on this subject has been frustrating due to our geographical location and limited resources."

Unfortunately NMAA's archive does not retain data on the time a question was transmitted or received; this would have yielded more specific data about submission times. In lieu of that, clients were asked to estimate the time they submitted the question, using six-hour segments. As Table 3 indicates, although about half of the respondents submitted questions during what approximated working hours (6 A.M. to 6 P.M.), a very high percentage submitted questions in the evening between 6 P.M. and midnight. Although public libraries may have reference assistance available in the evenings, museum and academic art libraries frequently do not. Museum libraries in particular may have limited hours and accessibility to the public. NMAA, for example, is generally open from 10:00 A.M. to 5:30 P.M. The latter findings indicate that the convenience of submitting questions outside normal reference service hours is an important aspect of the service to the respondents in this survey.

Table 3. Time of day questions were submitted

Time	Number (N)	Percentage (%)
Morning (6 A.M. to noon)	7	19
Afternoon (Noon to 6 P.M.)	12	32
Evening (6 P.M. to midnight)	17	46
Night (Midnight to 6 A.M.)	1	3
Total	37	100

Note. Based on respondents who received answers or messages asking for additional information. (N=37)

Place of Q&A Service in Normal Information Gathering

With digital reference services as convenient as they are, the question arises as to whether clients are moving immediately to these services or whether they are incorporating them into other information gathering related to the question. Table 4 begins to answer this question. Only a few (four, 8 percent) of the clients moved directly to the digital reference service without any previous attempts to answer the question, whereas nine (17 percent) indicated that they had used four or more sources. On average, the respondents used 2.2 other sources (standard de-

Table 4. Actions taken prior to submitting query

Action	Number (N)	Percentage (%)
Nothing	5	9.4
Checked in own books	26	49.1
Consulted a friend	14	26.4
Consulted a local museum/curator	16	30.2
Checked in a bookstore	14	26.4
Consulted a local library/librarian	24	45.3
Checked the Internet	14	26.4
Other	19	35.8

Note. Percentage is percentage of respondents taking that action (N=53); the percentages do not add up to 100 because respondents could indicate more than one action.

viation 1.4) before they approached NMAA's digital reference service. About half said they had checked their own books and/or a local library. Slightly less than one third indicated they consulted either a local museum or a friend or had checked in a bookstore. About one third indicated they had done other things; most indicated checking the Web.

Table 5 shows the subsequent actions taken by the respondents who did not receive a response or whose response consisted of a referral and/or solicitation of additional information ($N=22$). Five (23 percent) did nothing; the others took an average of 1.6 (standard deviation .9) actions when no response was received. Only three (14 percent) re-submitted the question, indicating that requests for follow up rarely result in replies. The others took a variety of actions, with more opting for consulting a local library or librarian and/or checking the Internet than for consulting others or checking their own collections.

Effectiveness of the Service

The sample included a mixture of responses and nonresponses (i.e., the 37 percent of the total sample that received no response

Table 5. Actions taken subsequently by those receiving no response or response without answer

Action	Number (*N*)	Percentage (%)
Nothing	5	23
Resubmitted question	3	14
Checked in own books	2	9
Consulted a friend	2	9
Consulted a local museum/curator	3	14
Checked in a bookstore	2	9
Consulted a local library/librarian	6	27
Checked the Internet	4	18
Other	6	27

Note. Percentage is percentage of respondents in these categories taking that action (*N=22*); the percentage do not add up to 100 because respondents could indicate more than one action.

because of the volume of questions received). The digital reference service responded to 222 (63 percent) of the 355 messages in the original sample. Of the 222 responses, 144 (65 percent) provided an answer to the question and 78 (35 percent) asked for additional information about the question or referred the client elsewhere. Figures 7 and 8 show an example of each type of response. Because of the volume of questions received, 133 (37 percent of total sample) received no response. At the time, NMAA was not providing an automatic acknowledgment of the query to the client upon receipt, so the latter group literally received no response whatsoever from the system. The questionnaire was the first system-initiated response based on that particular query.

The questionnaire asked the client to rate the effectiveness of the specific response by two general measures: satisfaction and usefulness. These measures were not defined and the client could interpret them according to his own perception. The satisfaction measure could be interpreted as meeting the client's expectations for the answer; a judgment of usefulness is probably based on subsequent use and may have been influenced by problems in phrasing of the question as well as in inadequacies in responding to the question as asked. The study also looked at clients' perceptions of specific characteristics of the response to their query: readability, thoroughness, authority of the information provided, and reasonableness of the response time. The way in which these variables were operationalized is indicated in the measure column in Table 6. Reasonableness of response time was clarified by asking the clients to indicate their ideal response time.

In general the respondents receiving answers were highly positive about the responses they received from the service. In relation to specific characteristics of the responses (measures 3 through 6), the respondents rated them highly almost all of the time, ranging from 93 percent for authority to 100 percent for reading level. In the broader measures which relied on the client's own definition of relative vague terms, their judgments were still high (74 percent for usefulness; 84 percent for satisfaction), but the gap between these levels and the levels for the specific measures seems to indicate that other variables are en-

Figure 7. Example of a typical question/response

DATE: 10/20/97
NAME: [DELETED]
EMAIL ADDRESS: [DELETED]
SUBJECT: William Bonnell (1804-1865)
QUESTION: I am interested in any advice on researching the artist William Bonnell. I am interested in finding out anything about him - thus far i have discovered nothing (except brief bio info.). Where did he paint? Where trained, etc. . . . I am working from a trio of paintings at the Art Institute of Chicago by Bonnell - the curators there have no information on him. Any assistance would be greatly appreciated.
SOURCES CONSULTED: Curatorial files, American Arts department, Art Institute of Chicago. American Sculptors active in 1800s dictionary
LEVEL: Higher Education
TIME: Two weeks
RESPONSE: Dear [DELETED], You asked about William Bonnell. I found one brief biographical entry in THE NEW YORK HISTORICAL SOCIETY's DICTIONARY OF ARTISTS IN AMERICA 1564-1860 by George C. Groce and David H. Wallace (New Haven, CT: Yale University Press, 1957); "Bonnell, William. Portrait painter known for portrait of Mary Wolverton Bray . . . now owned by the Historical Society of Hunterdon County, Flemington, N.J."

I also checked the Inventory of American Paintings Executed Before 1914, a large research database accessible on the Web (http://www.siris.si.edu; select "Search SIRIS catalogs;" select "Art Inventories." The Inventory is a census of American paintings in public and private collections and each listing is described with the following information: artist, title of work, date of execution, medium, subject, owner's name and address (if known), bibliographic references to the work. The Inventory lists 10 works by Bonnell, including the 3 at the AIC. I suggest you look at these, track the publications cited, and contact other museums with works by the artist (perhaps the curatorial offices at other museums have unearthed additional information).

I further checked the Catalog of American Portraits, a large research database project of the National Portrait Gallery. The Catalog, also accessible on the Web (http://www.npg.si.edu; select "Search") is a listing of portraits of significant Americans in public and private collections. The Catalog lists 2 works by Bonnell, and I'm certain you will want to look at these as well.
[DELETED name of librarian-respondent]

Figure 8. Example of referral or additional information response

DATE: 09-18-97
NAME: [DELETED]
EMAIL ADDRESS: [DELETED]
SUBJECT: Information on a Artist
QUESTION: I recently bought a framed picture by a artist who is from Montana I think,his name is Bill O'niel I am not sure what or how this picture (a bear coming over a ridge after a trapper on horse back is made of?? I am interested in finding out what I can about him and his work. It is really very interesting and any help if you can would be great and I thank you for your time!
SOURCES CONSULTED: This is the first place!
LEVEL: Higher Education
TIME: One month
RESPONSE: Dear [DELETED], You wrote: "I recently bought a framed picture by a artist who is from Montana I think, his name is Bill O'niel I am not sure what or how this picture (a bear coming over a ridge after a trapper on horse back is made of?? I am interested in finding out what I can about him and his work. It is really very interesting and any help if you can would be great and I thank you for your time!" Before I can research your question, I wonder if you can clarify it. If the painting you bought is signed, please look at the signature closely with a magnifying glass. It is important that I have the correct spelling of the name. The most likely spelling of the surname is "O'Neil" or "O'Neill" not "O'niel." What makes you think the artist is from Montana? I found a contemporary artist--William O'Neil--listed in WHO'S WHO IN AMERICAN ART, but he is Canadian. Did you purchase the painting at auction from a gallery or from the artist himself? Is the artist contemporary? Get back to me, and I'll see what I can do.
[DELETED name of librarian-respondent]

---

tering into their judgments at this point, not necessarily those identified by the authors of this study. As a whole, they judged the answers as thorough enough to answer the question adequately; readable enough so they could understand them; authoritative (based on their judgment of the sources used); and received within an acceptable time frame. However, some found the responses still were not entirely satisfactory, nor were they as useful as they wanted.

Table 6. Measures of effectiveness of the specific response and service

No.	Measure	Number (*N*)	Percentage (%)
	Based on Specific Response		
1	Satisfaction: Number and percentage rating highly (4–5 on 5-point scale)	26	84
2	Usefulness: Number and percentage rating highly (4–5 on 5-point scale)	23	74
3	Reading level: Number and percentage indicating response was "written at a level you could understand"	31	100
4	Thoroughness of response: Number and percentage indicating response was "thorough enough to answer the question adequately"	29	94
5	Authority of information provided: Number and percentage expressing high comfort level with the authority of the information, based on the documentation provided (4–5 on 5-point scale)	29	94
6	Response time: Number and percentage indicating that the response was "received within an acceptable amount of time" (*N*=37)	31	100
	Based on Overall Interactions with System		
7	Willingness to recommend: Number and percentage indicating yes (*N*=53)	45	87

Note. Most judgments are based on the respondents receiving answers to their questions (*N*=31, 59 percent of respondents). This figure is used as the percentage base for measures 1–5. The percentage for measure 6 is based on this group plus the additional group of those receiving referrals or solicitations of additional information. Measure 7 is based on all groups. If the *N* increases for a measure, it is included in the measure column.

Their verbal comments often reiterated the characteristics noted in the question:

1. "The answer was clear, precise, prompt, and complete."
2. "A lot more quick, responsive, and authoritative than searching in my local library, either through a reference librarian or on my own."
3. "Your program and response greatly exceeded our expectations is applauded."

In the latter example, the reference to expectations is interesting. In measuring service quality, one method looks at the gap between performance and expectations (P–E) (White, 1997: 4–5). Clients tend to regard service quality as high when performance exceeds expectations or, if performance is lower than expectations, when the gap between the two is small. Level of expectations is not always a major factor, but the gap between the two is. In the second verbal comment above, it is clear that the client's expectations influenced his satisfaction judgment. Unfortunately, there is no evidence indicating his expectations or the basis on which they were established.

As Table 7 indicates, only 3 percent required a one-day response; 45 percent would have been satisfied with three days or less; 81 percent with seven days or less; 94 percent with two weeks or less; and 100 percent with a month or less. NMAA's average response rate for the respondents' queries cannot be computed from the information in the archives.

All of the respondents receiving an answer were willing to recommend the service, even if the response simply asked for clarification or referred the client to another service. Of those who did not receive an answer (*N*=16), only nine (56 percent) were willing to recommend the service. The relatively low response rate from the latter group is probably also symptomatic of dissatisfaction with the service. Those not willing to recommend the service expressed their dissatisfaction in their comments:

1. "The lack of any response led me to delete the bookmark that I had created."

Table 7. Acceptable response times according to all respondents

Response Time	Number (*N*)	Percentage (%)
1 day	3	6
3 days or less	7	13
7 days or less	19	36
2 weeks or less	22	42
1 month or less	2	3

Note. Based on all respondents (*N*=53).

2. "I am responsible for my university's electronic reference desk. Commitment is essential. If service is arbitrary, forget it!"

Another suggested that "a confirmation e-mail should be sent when the question is received/looked at in order to specify a response time period, and to reassure those who sent the questions that their e-mails weren't lost in cyberspace and are actually being looked at by human beings." NMAA has recently added this response feature to their system.

CONCLUSION

Since the response rate was so small, the findings should be viewed with some skepticism. They can be summarized, however, as follows:

Characteristics of Users and Service Use

- Women used the service more than men.
- The clients used the service infrequently—for most clients, it was the only time they had used the service within the period of a year.
- The heaviest six-hour period during the day for transmitting requests occurred after regular office hours—between 6:00 P.M. and midnight, although about 50 percent of the questions were sent during the 12-hour period (6:00 A.M. to 6:00 P.M.) that represented normal working hours.

- Through this service, NMAA is indeed expanding its clientele beyond local users; it attracted users from 28 states and three foreign countries. Comments indicated that before using the service, some users had felt limited by local resources or a lack of mobility.

Integration of Digital Reference Service into Information Seeking Behavior

On average, the respondents had used two other sources before they approached the NMAA's reference desk; about half had consulted a local library. Slightly fewer had consulted a local museum or bookstore, a friend, or the Internet. Those receiving no response or a request for additional information took on average about 1.6 actions to continue looking for information but only 14 percent resubmitted their questions to NMAA.

Nature of Response

Of the clients in the overall sample (*N*=355), 41 percent (144) received an actual answer to their question, 22 percent (78) were asked for additional information, and 37 percent (133) received no response at all.

Effectiveness of Service

Those receiving information were generally satisfied and found the information useful. Most ranked the answers very high in terms of readability, thoroughness of response, authority of the information provided, and response time.

The discrepancy between the ranks for the specific ratings and the overall ratings indicates, however, that other factors entered into overall judgments. Because the overall judgments were rated lower, it is assumed that the other factors were judged more negatively than those considered in the sample.

Considering all respondents, including even those who received no response to their question, a very high percentage of the clients were willing to recommend the service to others. Not surprisingly, those who received no answer were more frequently negative. (Their negative feelings could have been ame-liorated, to some extent, through a simple acknowledgment of the question and indication of overload.)

These findings need to be validated through other studies because of the low response rate, but they are interesting nevertheless for insights into user behavior in relation to digital reference services. In the final report, the survey findings will be complemented by a thorough analysis of the queries and responses in the sample. The following comments focus on the methodology of the survey, indicating some of the problems addressed and the solutions that worked or did not work in this study.

Sample-related Problems

Difficulty of drawing a sample of users from a data archive in which the unit is the message, not the user: The data archive consisted of messages maintained by day with no index by user, so researchers had to draw the sample by day, then develop the sample of users from that sample. Fortunately there were few repeat clients in the archive. The researchers encountered no cases of repeat clients in the sample. Any studies wishing to emphasize repeat clients or responses to follow-up questions in the future will have to develop a means of indexing the questioner to identify the questioners submitting multiple messages.

Problem of children in the sample: The researchers wanted to avoid any parental concerns about eliciting information from children, so children were intentionally excluded from the original sample. To do this the researchers drew from educational level as indicated on the query form, supplemented by comments within the questions. This was a remarkably accurate way of identifying this subgroup. In addition, we included in the cover letter a comment indicating that if the person were under 18, he should indicate that on the questionnaire and return it without response. Only one questionnaire was returned by a parent with a comment to that effect.

Addressing the heterogenity of responses among the members of the sample: From the sample, it was apparent at a basic level the nature of the response provided to the clients: answers, requests for additional information, and no response. The researchers wanted to elicit information from all three groups. Some of the information could be obtained from all groups and some was response-specific, so the questionnaire was tailored to each respondent group. It contained a set of core questions and a set of variable questions based on the nature of the response.

Memory/Questionnaire Problems

Increasing the reliability and validity of the responses: Anytime a researcher asks an individual about an interaction that occurred at some time over the period of a year, there is the possibility that the respondent will not remember the encounter accurately and will generalize all encounters with that service and others. In this study, researchers used a critical incident technique (i.e., researchers identified a specific encounter and asked questions about that encounter). To refresh the respondent's memory, a copy of the question and response was included with the questionnaire. This allowed researchers to ask more specific questions and to ensure that the answers related to the incident as much as possible.

Operationalizing the effectiveness judgments: Effectiveness is a multifaceted concept. In this study, for those receiving responses, effectiveness was operationalized through several different judgments. Two overall judgments of satisfaction and usefulness and four specific judgments—readability, thoroughness, authority of the information provided, and reasonableness of the response time—were based on the actual response. One additional judgment, willingness to recommend, was based on overall interactions with the service and was answered by all categories of respondents.

Eliciting Information via E-mail

Volatility of e-mail addresses: People change their e-mail addresses when they move to a different Internet service provider or otherwise change accounts. In this study, 80 (23 percent) of the questionnaires were returned immediately because the respondent no longer existed at that address. In the future, the sample should be drawn sufficiently large so that substitutes can be made for sample members with address problems.

Electronic mail software that does not support questionnaires or respondents who do not know how to respond to a questionnaire online: In this study, a simple questionnaire was added to the cover letter and respondents were asked to reply. The questionnaire was within the message, not attached to it as a separate file. The questions were phrased so that a person, in many cases, could opt to reply by including the original message, and simply marking an "X" or "Yes" or "No" after the question, and perhaps writing a brief comment. Some e-mail software programs did not allow that option or the respondent did not know how to use the reply feature with the message included. In some cases, respondents simply replied by giving the number of the question and a brief response or, in a few cases, printed out the questionnaire and mailed it in. There is no way of knowing how many potential respondents faced this problem and simply elected not to respond. An alternative is to offer respondents the option of receiving a questionnaire by postal mail with a return envelope. Another study seeking information from librarians offered this option recently; however, only one of ten respondents chose this alternative, although two printed the questionnaire and faxed their responses (Abels and Magi, forthcoming).

Misperceptions about length of questionnaire: The questionnaire appeared much longer than it was because of the cover letter with its enclosed question and response. The respondent had to scroll through several screens to actually reach the questionnaire. The misperception regarding the actual length of the questionnaire may have stemmed from the multiple screens and contributed to the poor response rate.

Response Rate

The researchers expected a higher response rate for several reasons: first, it was expected that clients who had received good service would respond out of good will; second, personalizing the letter and keeping the questionnaire brief should have encouraged response. The initial response rate was low, and a follow-up e-mail message two weeks later yielded very few additional responses. The limited amount of research on e-mail survey methodology sheds some light on the problem of low response rates. Schaefer and Dillman's (1998) study of e-mail surveys found that an e-mail pre-notice was necessary to boost e-mail response rates to the point where they equaled that of mail surveys. Mehta and Sivadas (1995) found unsolicited surveys were often unwelcome. In this study, several people returned the questionnaire with negative comments about unsolicited mail. Good will toward the institution for providing a service to them seemed nonexistent in some cases. For any e-mail survey in the future, a preliminary notice seems warranted, asking people to participate and sending questionnaires only to those responding positively. Again, this approach has implications for the sample.

CONCLUSION

This paper contributes to the literature related to digital reference in two ways. First, it reports on the use patterns of a digital reference service designed to expand access to the collections of a major art research library. As such, it is one of the few digital reference user studies reported in the literature. Second, the methodological comments provide guidance for others conducting studies of clients through the use of e-mail questionnaires and suggest constructive ways to increase the reliability and validity of the data and the response rate.

APPENDIX A

Cover Letter

We are conducting a study of the e-mail reference service offered by the National Museum of American Art to understand how digital reference is used and how e-mail questions on art are formulated. Your question was chosen randomly from the museum's archive of questions. Would you please help us by answering the brief, attached questionnaire (5–10 minutes) about your experience with the NMAA electronic reference service? To refresh your memory, your question and the response are noted at the beginning of the questionnaire.

By answering this questionnaire, we assume that you consent to participate in this study. All data used in this study are confidential, and your name will not be identified. The data you provide will be grouped with other data for reporting and presentation. Any specific examples will not be linked to an individual. There are no known risks to your participating in this research. The results will benefit the implementation of electronic reference services on the Internet. The research is undertaken with the support of the National Museum of American Art and the University of Maryland.

If you are under the age of 18, please do not answer this questionnaire, but return it. If you are not the person who submitted the question reproduced in this message, please forward the questionnaire to the person who did. If you cannot forward it, please return the questionnaire with a note to that effect. If you prefer, you may print out the message and questionnaire and return it to the address indicated below.

We appreciate your participation. Please feel free to contact Laura Sowers with any questions you may have about this research.

Laura Sowers and Marilyn Domas White, Associate Professor
College of Library and Information Studies
University of Maryland
Hornbake 4105, South Wing, Box 18
College Park, MD 20742
e-mail: *sowers@wam.umd.edu*

APPENDIX B

Variant Forms of the NMAA Electronic Reference Desk Study Questionnaire

In the first part of the questionnaire, please make your judgments only about the question and response indicated below, not about all your experiences with the electronic reference service.

[INSERT QUESTION AND RESPONSE]

[Note: At this point the variations occur. The three alternatives are included here with a preliminary indication of the client group receiving each.]

Variant 1: For Users with Response with Answer

1a. How satisfied were you with the answer? (1 not satisfied at all; 5 very satisfied)
1b. If you answered with a 1 or 2, please indicate why briefly.
2a. How useful was it? (1 not useful; 5 very useful)
2b. If you answered 1 or 2, please indicate why briefly.
3. Please answer each lettered part with either yes or no. If you answer no, please explain briefly. The followup questions for (c) and (d) should be answered as noted. Was the answer to your question:
   a. Written at a level you could understand?
   b. Thorough enough to answer the question adequately?
   c. Adequately documented?
      How comfortable did you feel with the authority of the information provided, based on this documentation? (1, not comfortable; 5, very comfortable)
   d. Received within acceptable amount of time?
      What did you consider an acceptable amount of time?
4. What had you done to answer this question before contacting NMAA? (Mark an X after all that apply.)
   a. Nothing
   b. Checked in my own books

    c. Consulted a friend

    d. Consulted a local museum/curator

    e. Checked in a bookstore

    f. Checked a local library/librarian

    g. Other (Please describe briefly.)

5. What time of day did you submit this question? (Mark only one.)

    a. Morning (6:01 A.M. to noon)

    b. Afternoon (12:01 P.M. to 6:00 P.M.)

    c. Evening (6:01 P.M. to midnight)

    d. Night (12:01 A.M. to 6:00 A.M.)

Now we would like to ask you about your general use of the NMAA service and about yourself.

6. How did you find out about the NMAA Electronic Reference Desk?

7. How many times have you used the service over the past year?

8. Would you recommend the service to anyone else?

9a. What is your gender?

9b. What state are you located in? If you are in a country outside the United States, indicate the country.

10. Please note any other comments about this question/answer or about the Electronic Reference Desk generally.

Variant 2: For Users with Response without Answer

The Electronic Reference Desk staff were unable to answer your question.

1. What did you do after this response? (Mark an X after all that apply.)

    a. Resubmitted question with additional information

    b. Nothing

    c. Checked in my own books

    d. Consulted a friend

    e. Consulted a local museum/curator

    f. Checked in a bookstore

    g. Consulted a local library/librarian

    h. Other (Please describe briefly.)

2a. Was the response received within an acceptable amount of time?

2b. What did you consider an acceptable amount of time?

3. What had you done to answer this question before contacting NMAA? (Mark an X after all that apply.)

    a. Nothing

    b. Checked in my own books

    c. Consulted a friend

    d. Consulted a local museum/curator

    e. Checked in a bookstore

    f. Consulted a local library/librarian

    g. Other (Please describe briefly.)

4. What time of day did you submit this question? (Mark only one.)

    a. Morning (6:01 A.M. to noon)

    b. Afternoon (12:01 P.M. to 6:00 P.M.)

    c. Evening (6:01 P.M. to midnight)

    d. Night (12:01 A.M. to 6:00 A.M.)

Now we would like to ask you about your general use of the NMAA service.

5. How did you find out about the NMAA Electronic Reference Desk?

6. How many times have you used the service over the past year?

7. Would you recommend the service to anyone else?

8a. What is your gender?

8b. What state are you located in? If you are in a country outside the United States, indicate the country.

9. Please note any other comments about this question/answer or about the Electronic Reference Desk generally.

Variant 3: For Users Who Did Not Receive a Response

The Electronic Reference Desk staff did not respond to your question.

1. What did you do when this became apparent to you? (Mark an X after all that apply.)
   a. Resubmitted question with additional information
   b. Nothing
   c. Checked in my own books
   d. Consulted a friend
   e. Consulted a local museum/curator
   f. Checked in a bookstore
   g. Consulted a local library/librarian
   h. Other (Please describe briefly.)
2. What had you done to answer this question before contacting NMAA? (Mark an X after as many as apply.)
   a. Nothing
   b. Checked in my own books
   c. Consulted a friend
   d. Consulted a local museum/curator
   e. Checked in a bookstore
   f. Consulted a local library/librarian
   g. Other (Please describe briefly.)
3. What time of day did you submit this question? (Mark only one.)
   a. Morning (6:01 A.M. to noon)
   b. Afternoon (12:01 P.M. to 6:00 P.M.)
   c. Evening (6:01 P.M. to midnight)
   d. Night (12:01 A.M. to 6:00 A.M.)

Now we would like to ask you about your general use of the NMAA service.

4. How did you find out about the NMAA Electronic Reference Desk?
5. How many times have you used the service over the past year?
6. Would you recommend the service to anyone else?

7a. What is your gender?

7b. What state are you located in? If you are in a country outside the United States, indicate the country.

8. Please note any other comments about this question/answer or about the Electronic Reference Desk generally.

NOTES

1. Editors' note: Since the writing of this paper, the name of the service has been changed to Ask Joan of Art (*www.nmaa.si.edu/referencedesk/*).
2. The response rate for each category of responses was computed based on the overall sample of 355, not the adjusted sample. They were: 22 percent for those whose questions were answered, 8 percent for those asked for additional information, and 12 percent for those receiving no response.

REFERENCES

Abels, Eileen G. 1996. "The E-mail Reference Interview." *RQ* 35, no. 3 (Spring): 345–58.

Abels, Eileen G. and T. Magi. (forthcoming). "Current Practices and Trends in 20 Top Business School Libraries." *Journal of Business & Finance Librarianship* 6 (3). (forthcoming 2001).

Fishman, Diane L. 1998. "Managing the Virtual Reference Desk: How to Plan an Effective E-mail Reference System." *Medical Reference Services Quarterly* 17, no. 1 (Spring): 1–10.

Hahn, Karla. 1997. An Investigation of an E-mail-based Help Service. CLIS Technical Report No. 97–03. College Park, Md.: College of Library and Information Services, University of Maryland.

Lankes, R. David. 1998. *Building & Maintaining Internet Information Services: K-12 Digital Reference Services.* Syracuse, N.Y.: ERIC Clearinghouse on Information and Technology.

Mehta, R. and E. Sivadas. 1995. "Comparing Response Rates and Response Content in Mail Versus Electronic Mail Surveys." *Journal of the Market Research Society* 37: 429–39.

Ryan, Sara. 1996. "Reference Service for the Internet Community: A Case Study of the Internet Public Library Reference Division." *Library & Information Science Research* 18, no. 3 (Summer): 241–59.

Schaefer, D. and D. Dillman. 1998. "Development of a Standard E-mail Methodology." *Public Opinion Quarterly* 62: 378–93.

Stahl, Joan. 1998a. Getting Underway: The Virtual Reference Desk at the National Museum of American Art. In *AskA Starter Kit: How to Build and Maintain Digital Reference Services,* by R. David Lankes and Abby S. Kasowitz. Syracuse, N.Y.: ERIC Clearinghouse on Information & Technology.

Stahl, Joan. 1998b. "'Have a Question? Click Here': Electronic Reference at the National Museum of American Art." *Art Documentation* 17: 10–12.

Still, Julie M. and Frank M. Campbell. 1993. "Librarian in a Box: The Use of Electronic Mail for Reference." *Reference Service Review* 21, no. 1: 15–18.

Tibbo, Helen R. 1995. "Interviewing Techniques for Remote Reference: Electronic Versus Traditional Environments." *American Archivist* 58: 294–310.

U.S. National Museum of American Art. 1998. Mission Statement. [Online.] Available: *http://nmaa-ryder.si.edu/nmaainfo/dept-director-mission.html* [November 6]

White, Marilyn Domas. 1997. Measuring Service Quality in Libraries. In *Advances in Library Administration and Organization*, edited by Delmus E. Williams and Edward D. Garten. Greenwich, Conn.: JAI Press, Inc.

White, Marilyn Domas, ed. 1999. Analyzing Electronic Question/Answer Services: Framework and Evaluations of Selected Services. CLIS Technical Report No. 99–02. College Park, Md.: College of Library and Information Services, University of Maryland.

Part V

Digital Reference Technology Spotlight

OVERVIEW

The first digital reference efforts were launched using e-mail as the primary communication technology. While many services today still employ e-mail, at least to some extent, other technologies are finding their way into the reference process, including chatroom technology, Web contact center software, and help desk solutions.

The papers in this section discuss specific technology solutions as applied to three digital reference services, two from academic libraries and one from a library consortium. The authors describe special software features, new policies resulting from technology-related processes, new aspects of service made possible by the technology, and plans for the future. In some cases, authors suggested improvements for the software products used.

These papers offer a sampling of digital reference services and tools. They illustrate successful integration of reference service and technology from three different perspectives. Most importantly, they stress the need to stay current with tools and products that can be used to facilitate and enhance the reference process.

Moving Reference to the Web

Susan McGlamery and Steve Coffman

This paper examines the practical details of setting up a live Web reference service based on the call center model. It describes a pilot project to provide live Web and phone reference services for 37 public libraries in the Southern California area, which is currently under development for the Metropolitan Cooperative Library System. The paper describes the basic system architecture and the various kinds of hardware and software that will be required to make it work; procedures for estimating the potential reference load the service would have to support; and methods for using special call center formulae to estimate the necessary number of staff and incoming phone lines. Finally, the paper provides detailed estimates of what it costs to design, develop, and operate this type of service.

INTRODUCTION

Libraries have tried to make reference services easier to access, whether by telephone, fax or e-mail, but these services do not fully take advantage of the immediacy and convenience of Web interaction. This paper will test the concept of using Web contact center software to offer reference assistance to remote users. Contact center software provides live interaction and collaborative tools, including call routing (to better network with subject specialists in remote locations) and collaborative browsing (allowing the reference librarian to guide the patron's browser to the appropriate URLs). The project described in this paper will purchase the Web contact center software, install it on a central server, and test it with a pilot group of public and academic libraries in Los Angeles and Orange Counties. Once the software is tested, these libraries will form the nucleus of a virtual reference network, which will provide immediate, point-of-need reference service to residents of Los Angeles and Orange Counties, available at all times and from all locations.

It may be true that "[t]he beginnings of reference service are lost in antiquity" (Rothstein, 1955: 20), but formalized reference services have been an integral part of American libraries since the last quarter of the nineteenth century. At the first American Library Association conference in 1876, librarians were urged to disseminate information actively, rather than to merely collect materials (Rothstein, 1955). Since that time, reference librarians have utilized the latest technologies to ensure that information seekers get what they need, in the most convenient method possible. The dream, naturally, is to provide reference assistance at that point in time when the researcher needs the information. To achieve this, librarians have offered their services in many modes, including the U.S. mail, telephone, fax, e-mail, and library Web pages, all in an attempt to bring the reference librarian to the researcher, and thus enhance the value of the reference transaction. But are the researchers of today who simply go to the library's Web page receiving the same quality of reference service that they would have received one hundred years ago by walking up to the reference desk? Although much has been gained, has something been lost?

EXPERIMENTS WITH REFERENCE ON THE WEB

It is almost a cliché to state that the Internet has brought new challenges along with new opportunities. Today researchers have access to more information at their desktops than was contained in an entire library fifty years ago. Librarians have been quick to adopt the Internet to meet customer demand; even before the advent of the World Wide Web, the Library of Congress and many university libraries set up gopher sites that organized Internet resources by subject. Now the gopher sites have become Websites, but the best of them still fulfill the same mission: to provide a useful subject directory of Internet resources, selected, and evaluated by librarians (e.g., Librarians' Index to the

Internet, *www.lii.org*). Although these sites provide an excellent foundation for self-help (research conducted by the user without a librarian's assistance), they do not provide the same quality of service as that obtained at the reference desk: the researcher can't ask a question.

One obvious solution is for the library to attach an e-mail form to its subject directory, thus providing a means for researchers to obtain information not found on the library's Web page. A recent survey of public libraries in Los Angeles County revealed that 40 percent of the libraries were offering some form of e-mail reference service.[1] Some e-mail reference sites exist apart from physical libraries, such as the Internet Public Library (*www.ipl.org*), and AskERIC (*www.askeric.org*). The Virtual Reference Desk maintains a collection of records of such services in the AskA+ Locator (*www.vrd.org/locator/subject.html*). Although these services do provide a mechanism for users to ask questions, the transaction does not contain the same qualities as the face-to-face interaction with a reference librarian. First, the response is not immediate. Typically, the user must wait at least one hour, and sometimes up to two weeks, to get a response. Also, those who have tried to do a reference interview using e-mail know that the lack of interactivity can require numerous transactions. This is not to assert that e-mail reference has no place; on the contrary, it works quite well for those who do not need a response immediately, and, in the case of AskA services, to access experts who would otherwise be unavailable. E-mail also provides opportunities to ask questions that one might not be comfortable asking in a face-to-face situation.

In order to approach the qualities of real time reference, librarians have moved beyond subject directories and e-mail, and have experimented with new technologies, such as chat, NetMeeting, and CU-SeeMe. Although these technologies provide live one-on-one interaction between the librarian and the researcher, they do not scale for the Web. CU-SeeMe and other video technologies require researchers to have certain equipment (usually cameras and microphones) before they can access the services. This is not a problem within the library, or from a central library site to a branch, but it can be problematic for remote users at home, off-campus, or anywhere other than the library. Another potential problem arises if more than one researcher attempts to contact the library at the same time. There is no queuing or routing mechanism inherent in these solutions, thus reducing scalability for the Web.

WEB CONTACT CENTER SOFTWARE

Where do we go from here? It is often instructive to look outside the profession to see what the private sector does in analogous situations. Librarians are not the only ones who answer questions. Today many companies have centralized customer service or customer support call centers to handle product sales and service. The staff in these centers may handle thousands of questions per hour ranging from simple inquiries such as "What's my account balance?" at a banking call center, to the more complex questions such as "My child is running a fever. Should I bring her in for a doctor's visit?" Admittedly, the questions handled by a typical customer support center differ significantly from the types of questions handled at a reference desk; libraries handle a much broader range of questions than are answered in most commercial call centers. Nevertheless, companies do spend a significant amount of money on customer service and are therefore interested in any technology that will make question handling more satisfying to the customer, as well as more cost-effective for the company.

The Internet has not only brought radical changes to the way librarians access information; it has also affected the way consumers make purchasing decisions. For instance, Jupiter Communications recently reported that more than 80 percent of U.S. online consumers trust online news as much as they trust newspapers, broadcast TV, and cable news outlets (How the Web, 1999). Companies are quick to note these changes in customer preference. Of course the private sector has a real incentive to exploit the power of the Internet: not only is it more cost-effective to provide customer support online than via telephone call centers (Coffman, 1999; Coffman and Saxton, 1999), but consumers are increasingly choosing online as the most convenient way to shop.[2] Therefore, the private sector has a compelling interest in providing effective, scalable customer service over the Web.

Inevitably, software developers have crafted a solution: Web contact center software. The software performs the same functions as telephone call centers, thus retaining the same efficiencies, but also takes advantage of the new possibilities offered by the Web. A telephone call center typically has two layers between the customers calling in and the agents who answer the questions: an IVR system (Interactive Voice Response) and an ACD (Automated Call Distribution). The IVR provides automated information according to the selections made by customers using their telephone keypad ("Press 1 for locations; press 2 for your account balance . . . "); the ACD handles those requests that the IVR can't satisfy (when the customer needs to speak with a live person). Companies try to set up IVRs to handle as many of the incoming calls as possible (many centers find they can answer 80 percent or more of the calls with an IVR), leaving the ACD to route the remaining calls that require live assistance to the next available, and most appropriate, agent.

When moving to a Web-based solution, companies do not want to forego the efficiencies inherent in the IVR/ACD model. Instead of an IVR, companies rely on their Website to provide the most commonly requested information. If the customer still needs help, the software must provide the function of an ACD, such as queuing of incoming requests and routing to the next available agent. The routing is defined by rules set up by the company. For example, all requests for advice on home loans can go to the home loan experts, and all requests for car loans can be routed to the car loan experts.

The Web contact center software provides the same functionality as the telephone call centers, through queuing and routing, but it also takes advantage of the expanded opportunities inherent in the Web. The Web provides a variety of ways to handle live contact with the customer, and the software takes advantage of all of these. With a Web-based solution, the customer initiates contact by going to the company's Website and clicking on a help button. The software can be configured to allow a combination of e-mail, chat, call back, voice over IP, and even video. The call back feature is used by companies such as Lands' End (*www.landsend.com*) and is specifically designed for customers with a phone line (or cell phone) in addition to their Internet connection. Using the software, the customer requests a call back from a Lands' End agent, thus allowing the agent and the customer to talk while viewing the same Web pages together.

In addition to the expanded communication possibilities, the software takes full advantage of collaborative tools such as pushing (delivering information to the user), form filling, and taking control of the requestor's browser. This has many exciting possibilities for libraries. Here's an example of how a reference transaction could occur in a library that uses Web contact center software such as that used on the Lands' End site.

User Scenario

Jane is an entrepreneur who wants information on how to start a business. She doesn't want to drive to the library and look for parking, so she sits at home and accesses the library's Website. The library's Web page has an icon that says, "Click here to talk to a librarian." Jane dutifully clicks on the icon, where she has a choice of sending the library an e-mail (if she doesn't need a response right away), opening up a chat session, or, if she has access to another phone line, getting the librarian to call her right back. Jane selects the chat session.

Once Jane initiates the chat, she is asked for some information to identify herself, such as her name and e-mail address. The library can also request that Jane type in her library card number, if it wishes to allow access only to registered users. Once Jane has logged onto the session, she receives a message that says, "A librarian will be with you shortly. In the meantime, perhaps you'd be interested in finding out more about the Library." This feature is called "pages on hold," and allows the library to set up a preprogrammed list of URLs or other information to push to Jane's browser while she is waiting (as opposed to the music one hears in a telephone transaction).

The software queues Jane's request, which is then routed according to rules that the library has established. For example, all requests coming in on the library's business Web page will be routed to the business librarians; requests coming in through the children's site go to different staff.

Once a librarian receives the question, the software provides a variety of tools to assist in the answering process. For example, the software allows scripting, so the business library can set up a hierarchical script based on the most commonly asked business questions, which is then available to any librarian in answering these requests. If Jane is asking a common question, like "how do you start a business?," the librarian could script a generic answer in advance and simply push it to Jane's browser. The answer could be in the form of a Web page, a PowerPoint presentation, a list of frequently asked questions (FAQ), or any other electronic resource available to the library. The script could also contain basic greetings from the librarian, as well as the closing statement, "Please let me know if you need anything further."

If Jane's question is more detailed (e.g., how many pet shops are in Los Angeles County), the librarian may elect to show Jane how to search a business database to find this information. Assuming the library has access to such a database on its Website, the librarian can initiate "follow me browsing." This feature allows the librarian to take control of Jane's browser to lead Jane through each step of the process: finding the databases on the library's Website, selecting the right database, filling in the search form for Jane, then pushing the results of the search.[3] If Jane has problems searching a database, the librarian can select "form share" to see what Jane has entered in the database search form. Thus the librarian will know if Jane misspelled a word or is in the wrong database.

Once Jane indicates that she has all she needs, she will receive an e-mail transcript containing the entire chat session as well as the URLs that were pushed. A copy of this transcript is also sent to the library. Now the library can see exactly what questions were asked, how they were answered, how many questions came in and when. We can use this information to staff the reference desk, train new staff, and to build our Websites, to enable more self-help. The software also maintains detailed statistics on all Web transactions and allows libraries to generate a variety of reports based on this data, such as the total number of questions, average length of time spent per question, questions by subject matter, busiest hours of the day, and so on.

Of course, Jane may not find the information she needs. Her question may relate to an area outside the librarian's expertise, such as patent searching or export regulations. In this case, the librarian can transfer the request to a subject specialist in patents or export regulation, just as one would transfer a phone call. If the subject specialist is not logged onto the system at the time, the request can be transferred by e-mail. Regardless of how the call is transferred, the referring librarian can send the transcript along, to make it easier for the expert to know what's happened so far and provide better service for Jane.

HOW LIBRARIES MIGHT USE THE SOFTWARE

The Web contact center software works well for companies, but can it work for libraries? Arguably, a model based on a telephone call center alone would not be particularly useful for libraries, because only a small percentage of reference questions come in through the telephone, and because it is difficult for the librarian and the patron to share content over the phone.

But the Internet changes all of that. Now, many of the resources used to answer questions are Web-based, or electronic (such as proprietary databases or library OPACs) and can be shared online with the patron. The Web is quickly becoming a large part of libraries' reference collections, so the Web contact center may become a viable model for providing reference services on the Internet.

There are a variety of ways libraries might be able to take advantage of this software to improve the way reference services are provided. Perhaps the simplest application would be to allow patrons to use the software to do unassisted collaborative browsing among themselves on the library Website. Lands' End has pioneered something similar to this on its catalog Website. This feature, called "Shop With Me," allows friends to meet each other online, log on to a collaborative session, and shop together on the Lands' End site. Each party can "show" the other interesting Web pages they have found, and either party can take the lead in guiding the other through the site. The two Web users can talk with each other using chat or telephone (if they have a second line available). The library could use a similar feature that permits users to browse the library's Website, various databases and other electronic resources together. This approach would allow libraries to experiment with this new technology with a minimum impact on existing reference staff and processes.

Another obvious use for the Web contact center software would be to help provide live reference services to the multitude of Web catalog terminals, Internet PCs, and other electronic workstations that are now in many library buildings. Much of the real research and catalog searching that goes on in libraries today is conducted by patrons hunched over PCs and Internet terminals that are often far removed from the regular reference desk. Patrons who run into trouble with a search are often loath to leave their machines and ask for help for fear that somebody will take their place, or that the search they have been working on for the past 10 minutes will just vanish from the screen. One way to address this problem would be to offer live reference assistance right on the catalog screen, so that when patrons run into trouble, they can just click on the button and speak or chat with a librarian without leaving the terminal. It is possible that the librarian who handles that request could be sitting at the reference desk on the other side of the room, but it is also possible that the librarian might be sitting in a centralized catalog information center many miles away. In fact, in a large multibranch system, it is not hard to imagine that a small number of librarians could provide catalog assistance to all of the branches from a single centralized information center. This model might also work effectively for many academic libraries where catalog terminals and reference workstations may be scattered in subject libraries and other buildings throughout campus.

We could also use the software to provide more convenient and comprehensive reference services between a central library and its branches. A large number of major public and academic libraries are structured after the central/branch model, where the central library holds the in-depth reference collection and the staff who know how to use it, while the branches maintain basic reading collections. But it has never been easy for patrons in the branch locations to take advantage of the staff expertise and reference collections at the central library without actually going there (which, in a place like Los Angeles, can involve many miles of travel and hours of wasted time). The Web contact center software could offer at least a partial solution to this problem. If the software is available on reference terminals in the branches, patrons could get direct access to the specialized staff at the central library, and could take advantage of collaborative browsing and other tools to help them find the information they need.

A VIRTUAL REFERENCE NETWORK

If libraries can use the software to link between a central library and its branches, they could also use it to link to other resource libraries outside the system. This could lead to the development of a reference network that joins subject specialists and resource collections all over the world. The ready availability of Web content and the ability to share that content with patrons and others on the network in real time may facilitate sharing of reference services and questions with other institutions. In fact, if this software proves successful, a marketplace for reference services could develop over the network, in which some libraries make reference "programming" available to others, while other libraries purchase "programming" needed to provide the services their patrons want. The marketplace might work much like the PBS network: a Boston station develops programming and sells it to other stations on the network for rebroadcast in their communities. Similarly, a library in New York could develop a high-quality business reference service for its patrons and then re-sell it to libraries all over the world through the network. If the small rural library in Bishop, California decides to subscribe to that business service, its patrons automatically have access to world-class staff and resources that Bishop would not be able to develop alone. The PBS station in Bishop can broadcast a program like *The Civil War* to its viewers, even though it could never have developed the program itself. How would such a network really work? Who would pay for it and how? These and many other issues remain to be resolved; however, Web content and the Web contact center software make such a network at least conceivable for the first time. That in itself is a quantum leap from how we have thought about reference in the past.

The potential demand for convenient, live reference services over the Web could be many times what libraries currently are experiencing at the reference desk, if we truly came up with a service our patrons wanted and were brave enough to let them know about it. For example, it is estimated that 43 percent of the population in Los Angeles County has access to the Web from their home, school, or office. If all of these people logged on and asked an average of one additional question each, it would more than double the reference load at the County of Los Angeles Public Library, and require double the staff, double the resources, and double the money. Those with long experiences in the library field know that that is not likely to happen. So, in order to handle significant increases in service demand, librarians must find better and more efficient ways of doing reference.

Some of the tools that will be needed for this job are already available. The Web contact center software, for example, allows use of a much more efficient centralized staff which can be more closely tailored to the level of questions we anticipate than the "one or two warm bodies behind every reference desk" approach currently used to staff reference services. Similarly, networked reference services and improved access to outside experts could improve efficiency, as can be testified by librarians who have ever struggled to answer a question in an area they knew nothing about. However, there is much work to be done. In particular, it is necessary to explore ways to take advantage of Web self-help resources to anticipate and answer the most commonly asked questions up front, just as commercial counterparts have. It is necessary to take a closer look at tiered reference services such as the Brandeis model, which have not always worked well in physical library buildings, but may work much better in an electronic environment where transferring a question is much easier. Call centers, after all, have used tiered staffing models for years successfully. Finally, it is necessary to explore, evaluate, and, where appropriate, take advantage of all of the tools, techniques, and approaches others in the educational, nonprofit, government, and commercial sectors have developed to help them answer their customers' questions more effectively and efficiently.

PROOF OF CONCEPT

Previous discussions have presented concepts in the abstract, because until now, no library has actually used Web contact center software in any real reference applications. That is about to change.

The Metropolitan Cooperative Library System/Santiago Library System Consortium[4] recently received a Federal Library Services and Technology Act grant from the California State Library to purchase contact center software and test its applicability for reference. Out of the over 50 companies offering Web contact center software in 1999, the project chose Webline (recently acquired by Cisco), because it had the only product that met all of the project's criteria. As part of the project, at least three public libraries and one academic library within Los Angeles and Orange Counties will test the software and use it to provide reference assistance to their users. In addition, the pilot libraries will establish a fledgling reference referral network, using the software to transfer requests. For example, the public libraries may transfer requests to the university's medical library, and the university may transfer requests to the public library's genealogy department. The first group of libraries will go "live" with the service during the spring and summer of 2000. By fall of 2000, the project plans to offer an after-hours service, so that each library on the network has the option of forwarding their after-hours calls to a centralized staff.

The project leaders envision that users will access this service through their local library's Web page. Each participating library will place an icon on its Web page that says "click here to talk to a librarian" (or something similar). Each library will decide where on its Website to place the icon. For example, the icon can be placed on the Web catalog page, staffed by paraprofessionals who assist patrons in finding books from the Web catalog. Another option is to place the icon on a Web page containing reference databases (such as UMI or GaleNet), staffed by someone adept at searching these databases. Each library will decide the location(s) of the icon, the staff who will be on hand to answer the questions, and what hours the staff will be available to answer the questions. The library can decide to have "live" assistance during certain hours and e-mail assistance during other times, or both can be offered simultaneously.

Each library will decide what to do with questions that cannot be answered by its staff on call. For example, requests could be transferred to a senior reference librarian on staff (either "live" or by e-mail), or to the MCLS Reference Center (a second-level reference center currently funded by the California Library Services Act) or to any other subject specialists that may eventually be networked. Once the after-hours service is implemented, each library will decide if requests that come in when the library is closed will be forwarded to the centralized after-hours staff, or if these requests will be captured in e-mail and answered by the library during its regular business hours. The important feature of this project is that each participating library will maintain as much control as possible regarding how it offers the service, and what staff it will use. There will be no centralized, competing product or Web page produced by this project; to use the software, users must come in through their library's Website.

Many libraries are interested in participating in the project, not only for the networking component, but also for the potential internal applications detailed previously. For example, some libraries will be using the software to assist users with the catalog and electronic resources inside their buildings. Others will try linking some of their branches with their central reference services.

Other libraries will be experimenting with using the software for training purposes, not only for their own staff but also for the public or students. The software has a "seminar" feature, which allows the librarian to broadcast information (such as a PowerPoint presentation) simultaneously to as many as 500 users.

One of the biggest challenges to doing live reference on the Web and in this project is to provide easy access to the public while ensuring that libraries are not overwhelmed with reference questions that may take hours to answer. The Web contact center software was developed in a commercial setting, where the model assumes that 80 percent of incoming requests will be handled by the company's Website (similar to the IVR model). Can 80 percent of a library's reference requests be adequately handled by the library's Web page? This is not known. But that is one of the key questions that the project will try to address. A portion of the grant funds has been allocated to develop a few content-rich Websites in key subject areas, and libraries on the network will be able to use these sites as part of their reference Web page. This may be done through co-branding, so that each library can place a project-developed Web product on the library's own Web page, modified according to each library's own needs and clientele. These sites are referred to as "reference front ends," and it is hoped that they will help answer a great many of the patrons' questions before they can be tempted to click on the "Talk to a librarian" button. The first areas to be developed will be a business Website, a search engine tutorial, and a homework help center. If the patron does "click through" to live help, library staff trained to use the resources on these key sites can answer the bulk of the questions. Any requests that fall outside the scope of these key areas may then be routed to a subject specialist, either within the library or on the network.

THE JURY IS STILL OUT

It will be some time before it's known whether the Web contact center software and this model of reference service will work effectively for libraries. Based on the experience in other industries, the promise appears very real indeed. If this approach lives up to its promise, and reference is moved to the Web, then we can finally achieve the dream of providing the same quality of reference service over the Internet that was previously available only at the reference desk. This will allow our patrons to access the library anyway, anyhow, or anywhere.

NOTES

1. The MCLS Reference Committee, a consortium of public libraries in Los Angeles County, conducted a survey entitled "Disembodied Reference" in June 1998. Of the 31 public library jurisdictions in MCLS, 25 responded to the survey. Of those 25, 10 libraries provided an e-mail reference service. This survey has not been updated.
2. According to a recent survey, there are two main reasons why increasing numbers of consumers are shopping online: it's quick and it's easy. The Shopping 2000 survey, conducted between December 23, 1998 and January 6, 1999, surveyed 1,300 regular Internet users nationwide. "Consumers Cite Convenience as Lure to On-line Shopping," *Discount Store News* 38 (19 April 1999): 20.
3. For access to information that requires authentication, such as proprietary databases, the software requires the end-user to authenticate, using whatever means the library has already established, such as a library card.
4. The Metropolitan Cooperative Library System (MCLS) is a multi-type library cooperative headquartered in Pasadena, California, consisting of 31 public library jurisdictions and 23 associate member libraries located throughout Los Angeles, Orange and Ventura Counties. The Santiago Library System (SLS) is a nine-member public library consortium located in Orange County that contracts with MCLS for reference, delivery, and administrative services.

REFERENCES

Coffman, Steve. 1999. "Reference as Others Do It." *American Libraries* (May): 32.

Coffman, Steve and Matthew Saxton. 1999. "Staffing the Reference Desk in the Largely-Digital Library." *The Reference Librarian* 66: 141.

How the Web. 1999. "How the Web Was Won: An Online Editor Says the Internet Is Shifting the Distribution of Media Forever." *Editor & Publisher* 3: 38.

Rothstein, Samuel. 1955. *The Development of Reference Services through Academic Traditions, Library Practice, and Special Librarianship*. Chicago, Association of College and Reference Libraries. Quoted in "Reference Services and Libraries," *Encyclopedia of Library and Information Science*, vol. 25 (New York: Marcel Dekker, 1978).

The University of North Texas Libraries' Online Reference Help Desk

Monika Antonelli and Martha Tarlton

This paper describes the University of North Texas Libraries' Online Reference Help Desk. Topics covered include: factors in the selection of the ConferenceRoom Personal Edition real-time Windows chat server software; staffing by and training of volunteers; comparison with telephone reference; the question-answering process; procedures followed by the user and staff "operator" in a reference transaction; marketing; and ideas for future improvements.

BACKGROUND

The University of North Texas, UNT, is a comprehensive doctoral granting university located approximately 35 miles north of the Dallas-Fort Worth Metroplex. The university serves a growing student population of over 26,000, many of them commuters, and has been a leader among colleges and universities in the Southwest in providing access to computing technology. Students search the libraries' electronic resources in the general access labs throughout the campus. The university rapidly is expanding its off-site and distance education course offerings. In the spring of 2000, UNT will be opening the University of North Texas System Center at Dallas, which will eventually become a separate campus.

All of these factors have presented new challenges and opportunities in providing reference service. While some off-site users continued to obtain reference assistance by telephone, it became apparent that there was a need to provide digital reference service. In 1997, the libraries' Humanities and Social Sciences Department implemented an e-mail reference service via the Web. This provides for the transmittal of quick, factual reference questions any hour of the day or night.

Since negotiating most reference questions requires more of a dialog between the user and the librarian, it was necessary to explore the use of synchronous technology, including MOO[1], chat, and video technology. While MOO technology provides a rich environment for users to explore, its learning curve was too steep to be practical in a service environment. Internet Relay Chat (IRC), a popular synchronized mode of communication on college campuses, was not possible either due to the removal of the IRC client from the libraries' UNIX server. Video reference was also considered but dismissed because the target population currently did not own the required equipment to use such a service.

SELECTION OF CHATROOM SOFTWARE

In designing the UNT Online Reference Help Desk, one goal was to reach the largest number of patrons possible. The decision to provide a help desk in a chatroom environment was based on the premise that this was a technology that many students were familiar with and would be able to use with little or no training. The target population would not have to purchase additional equipment or download special software to use the service. Patrons only require a computer with access to the UNT Libraries' Web pages and an Internet browser that supports Java applets. Equipment and software requirements for staff working the help desk were easy to fill. A librarian needs a computer with access to the UNT Libraries' Web pages and either a Java capable browser or an IRC client.

UNT has a LAN/PC Management Department responsible for maintaining the software used for the Online Reference Help Desk. With their input, the WebMaster ConferenceRoom Personal Edition software (*www.webmaster.com*) was selected. ConferenceRoom runs on a library Web server. Originally the software was loaded on a Pentium 200 with 64 RAM and was later moved to a Pentium 333 with 250 RAM. ConferenceRoom was selected based on several factors. First, ConferenceRoom is the market share leader in real-time Windows chat server software. Second, it offered the power of an IRC environment that the UNT libraries were able to support. Third, it supported the three most important features of the Online Reference Help Desk:

1. Private reference interviews with patrons
2. Ability to remove or "kick" patrons out if they behaved inappropriately
3. Ability to record transactions

Finally, the software was very affordable (only $99.00).

STAFFING

The Online Reference Help Desk is currently staffed by volunteers. The nine volunteers are from the libraries' Humanities and Social Sciences Department, where the service originated. Seven of the volunteers are librarians and two volunteers are full-time staff members. In setting up the service, it was decided that people who staffed the Online Reference Help Desk would not simultaneously staff the physical reference desk. The reasoning behind this was that communicating in a virtual environment is labor intensive. The librarian is totally immersed in the transaction with the patron. In addition, it was difficult in the Online Reference Help Desk for one person to work with more than two patrons at a time.

Training sessions were developed and conducted for help desk volunteers. During these training sessions, it was discovered that library volunteers new to chat technology encountered a learning curve. Although the ConferenceRoom software is relatively simple to use, it offers many options and commands.

ONLINE VS. TELEPHONE REFERENCE

The purpose of the UNT Online Reference Help Desk is to answer reference questions and assist patrons in a synchronous online environment. Answering questions in a chatroom environment is similar to doing telephone reference. Both formats work best for questions that can be answered quickly. In both environments, users must notify librarians when they need assistance (librarians cannot monitor the network as they can the reference floor), librarians must stay in close contact with users in order to report on progress, and it is sometimes possible to arrange for follow-up communication (e.g., e-mail, phone, fax, library visit).

However, there are several advantages to using the online help desk over the phone to answer questions. First, an online help desk can be more cost effective for distance education students. By using the online help desk, a patron can save himself the cost of a long distance telephone charge. Second, if a patron only has one phone line and needs step-by-step instructions in the online environment, a virtual help desk can provide this assistance simply by having both the patron and the librarian open a second browser window. By toggling back and forth between the online desk and the resource, the librarian can walk the user through an instruction request. Third, the online help desk is an excellent resource for the hearing impaired. Finally, those doing research on public terminals (e.g., in a campus computer lab) may not have easy access to a phone and may be reluctant to leave their computers. A virtual help desk allows a patron in this environment access to reference assistance and does not require him to leave his seat.

QUESTION-ANSWERING PROCESS

Patrons notify librarians they need help by clicking on the "Page a Librarian" button, which sends the page through the libraries' Web server to a UNIX server called "Mailhost," the UNT campus paging and e-mail system. Then "Mailhost" sends the page to both the Online Reference Help Desk pager and to an electronic mailbox. (The e-mail page allows us to track when patrons are accessing the Online Reference Help Desk after hours.)

One of the problems with paging systems is the lag time between the patron's sending of the page and the librarian's receiving of the page. Generally, it takes between two to three minutes for a page to come through. Sometimes, it can take six minutes or more. This time lag can be a barrier to patron/librarian interaction, in that when patrons do not get an immediate response from a librarian, they may leave without having the question answered.

One of the first tasks performed after a librarian logs in for a shift is to check to see how the pager is working. This is done by going to the Online Reference Help Desk and sending a page by clicking on the "Page a Librarian" button. The librarian then times how long it takes for the page to come through on the pager.

Once the lag time is established, the librarian posts a message to this effect on the "Topic" bar. This area is used to make announcements to patrons in the Online Reference Help Desk such as, "Pages are taking approximately 2 minutes to go through. Please be patient."

To access UNT's Online Reference Help Desk patrons can either set their browser to *www.library.unt.edu/admin/HelpDesk/helpdesk.htm*, or they can locate it on the UNT Libraries home page (*www.library.unt.edu*) in the yellow "Spotlight" section. Once there, the patron types a name (no more than nine alphanumeric characters with no spaces in between) and has the option to enter an e-mail address. The patron then clicks on the "Connect" button to enter the Online Reference Help Desk and then on the "Page a Librarian" link to call a librarian to help.

Staff Procedures

To connect to the staff side of the Online Reference Help Desk, the librarian runs the IRC client program, XIRCON. Upon launching XIRCON, the program immediately connects to the IRC server housing the Online Reference Help Desk. Once the librarian has connected to the server, she then needs to join the room or channel designated for the Online Reference Help Desk. (ConferenceRoom offers the option to create one or more channels or rooms.) To join or enter the Online Reference Help Desk channel called #helpdesk, the librarian types "/join #helpdesk" and a second window appears showing the contents of the channel #helpdesk.

Once in the channel, a panel displays a list of people (patrons and librarians) currently connected to the channel #helpdesk. The symbol "@" in front of a name indicates that the person has "Operator" status. The operator is the first person to enter the room. Additional staff members can be designated operators if the original operator grants operator rights to them.

Operator status is a level of administration that gives the librarian a certain amount of control over the specific channel. With it the operator can:

- Set a topic within the channel.
- Give or take away operator status to or from other users in the channel.
- Remove (kick) a user from the channel.
- Ban a user from the channel.
- Change properties within the channel (number of people who can be in the channel, secret channel, invite only, moderated, etc.).

Writing Responses

There is down time when a librarian is responding to a patron's question. The librarian can only answer as fast as she can type. Depending on typing speed, a response can take anywhere from a few seconds to a few minutes. When staffing the Online Reference Help Desk, one has to consider that people have different communication styles. Some people prefer to type the whole answer before posting it. Others find it helpful to type parts of the reply and send it. So instead of typing a whole paragraph of information, one would type a line and hit return, type another line and hit return, and so forth. The benefit to doing this is that the lag time is shorter and it lets the patron know that the librarian is responding to the question.

Patron Skills and Procedures

Although there are many things patrons can do when they are in the Online Reference Help Desk, the minimal amount they need to know in order to communicate effectively in the Online Reference Help Desk is:

- Enter the chat room
- Page a librarian
- Type and send their communication using the message box
- Quit

When users first come to the Online Reference Help Desk, they have to enter a name (either a real name or pseudonym) for identification. Users also have the option of entering their e-mail address. This is helpful, because sometimes reference questions can take more than a few minutes to answer, and sometimes the needed information is not readily accessible. Having the user's e-mail address allows the librarian to contact and send the user additional information at a later time.

Once in the Online Reference Help Desk, users type their messages in the text box and press the "enter" key to submit messages to the librarian. Users who are not familiar with chat technology sometimes do not realize the necessity of doing this in order to communicate with the librarian. If the librarian suspects, by a user's inactivity, that the user does not know how to enter or send a message, the librarian can prompt the user by sending instructions on using the Online Reference Help Desk.

Conducting and Logging Transactions

ConferenceRoom allows the librarian and the user to conduct a private reference transaction by sending a private message. A private message is a one-on-one conversation. Only the two parties participating can read the messages. To send a private message to a user, the librarian can use the "/msg" command in the communication window. The librarian types: /msg

<user's name><message>. Example: "/msg Kimberly Do you need some help?" Another option is to type the communication in a private message box. To respond privately the user must double click on the librarian's name to pull up his own private message box. If the librarian uses the "/msg" command rather than open a new window to talk privately, both participants must use the "/msg" command each time.

ConferenceRoom also allows the librarian to log transactions. If the librarian has enacted a "Whois" command, this information will be captured in the log for access at a later time. The librarian can also peruse the log, study the reference interview, and evaluate it.

Behavior Issues

Since the start of the service, there has not been any disruptive behavior from patrons, although this type of behavior is common in chatrooms. In case this does occur in the future, the operator has the ability to remove a user by "kicking" him out of the room. If a patron is kicked from a room he can re-enter. If there is a problem with a person coming back frequently and being disruptive, the ConferenceRoom software allows the operator to ban the person so he is unable to get back in. This command actually places the ban on the computer the person is using. (Patrons using public terminals can work around the ban by moving to another computer.)

Another option the ConferenceRoom software offers is a profanity filter. Since UNT has not had any problems with profanity, this option has not been enabled. This software feature allows the administrator to create a list of specific words to be filtered. The administrator can set up the filter to either not display the user's message if he types a word listed in the filter or to send the user an automatic message indicating that the user must rephrase the message. In either case, the software will not send any word included in the profanity filter to the communications window.

MARKETING THE SERVICE

Marketing is an ongoing process. To date, the most effective way of marketing this service has been using e-mail. In the fall of 1999, e-mail messages were sent to every faculty and staff member on campus. The initial response to the e-mail was excellent and usage statistics increased, but since then usage has dropped. One possible barrier to the service may be the hours the service was available. From May 17, 1999 to October 1, 1999 the Online Reference Help Desk was only open from 2:00 P.M. to 5:00 P.M. on Mondays through Fridays. Starting October 3, 1999 the hours expanded to 10:00 A.M. to 5:00 P.M., Mondays through Fridays. Since that time, service usage has increased.

In addition to sending e-mail to the faculty and staff on campus, the service was advertised on several UNT USENET groups; to faculty subscribed to the mailing list for WebCT, the software product UNT uses to provide distance education classes; to the campus newspaper, the *NT Daily* (through press releases); and to the UNT electronic bulletin board, a campus-wide television system that broadcasts ongoing messages. Through our marketing efforts, we received a write-up in *Benchmarks*, the monthly campus computing newsletter.

The option of being able to send an announcement to the 26,000 students at UNT recently became available. This will be done in the near future. It is likely that this will prove the most effective method of advertising the service.

CONCLUSION

A lot has been learned from staffing this service for over five months. There are many ideas for future improvements and enhancements, including evaluating other software (although ConferenceRoom has some wonderful features, we know that other vendors may have products that better address our needs) and removing barriers to the service to make it easier for patrons to use. Some of the things the UNT Libraries' Humanities and Social Sciences Department would like to be able to do in the future with the Online Reference Help Desk include:

1. Provide better information to patrons after hours—The service should send a message stating the desk is not open and providing the hours of operation when patrons try to enter the Online Reference Help Desk after hours. At this time when users page the service during off-hours, they see an option on the automatic answering page to send us an e-mail message. During the operation of this service, several people have used this form to submit their information requests.
2. Screen out users not affiliated with the UNT community.
3. Provide automatic paging when a patron enters the Online Reference Help Desk—This would eliminate the need for the librarian to rely on the patron's use of the paging button.

Finally, we would like to investigate the ability to partner with other libraries. The Online Reference Help Desk is a virtual environment that can be staffed anywhere. By working collaboratively with libraries in other parts of the world, it would be possible to provide virtual reference service twenty-four hours a day.

NOTES

1. A MOO is an environment where users can communicate with each other using text and objects. MOO is an acronym for MUD, Object-Oriented—MUD being a multi-user dungeon (or multi-user dimension).

Click on the Wizard for Help: Using Help Desk Software for Real-Time Reference

Saundra Lipton

The University of Calgary (Canada) Library offered a trial of electronic reference, called Wizard Service, via the World Wide Web for several weeks in the fall 1998 and winter 1999 terms. User surveys indicated strong support for the service. The following concerns were identified: for complex questions it is often preferable to talk to the researcher; clients often lost the Wizard conversation box when librarians sent them a Web page; conversation mode would be more effective as real-time or ICQ chat; there was a significant delay before the system indicated that a client had exited; and Web pages could not be sent from within a catalog/database search. Several sample screens are included, and a list of questions received is appended.

INTRODUCTION

Desktop access to information is a vision that the University of Calgary Library has been working toward for a number of years. With over 150 electronic indexes, a number of full-text resources as well as numeric and statistical data, the library has come a long way towards accomplishing this vision. While desktop access to resources is a very valuable service, it needs to be supported by a similar electronic reference service.

In the fall of 1997, the University of Calgary tested a help desk software product produced by Net Effect Systems[1] (*www.neteffect.com*). This offered possibilities for electronic reference service. Over the spring and summer of 1998, library staff successfully tested and trained on this software, now called NEware. A trial of real-time electronic reference was originally planned for early fall of 1998, but technical difficulties with hardware upgrade issues delayed the start-up of the trial. After increasing server memory, the hardware was brought up to the specification needed. The University of Calgary Library receives continuing support from Net Effect. Their product and technical support has been critical to the success of our efforts to introduce desktop reference services.

The trial of electronic reference (called Wizard Service) was offered from November 12 to December 9, 1998 and February 8 to April 15, 1999. The picture on the University of Calgary Library home page was replaced with an image of a Wizard (Figure 9); clicking this image connected researchers to real-time electronic reference assistance (Figure 10). This service was offered Monday through Thursday from 4 P.M. to 8 P.M. Eight library reference staff members were involved in providing this service, and most shifts were staffed by one person. Software

Figure 9. Library home page for the winter trial

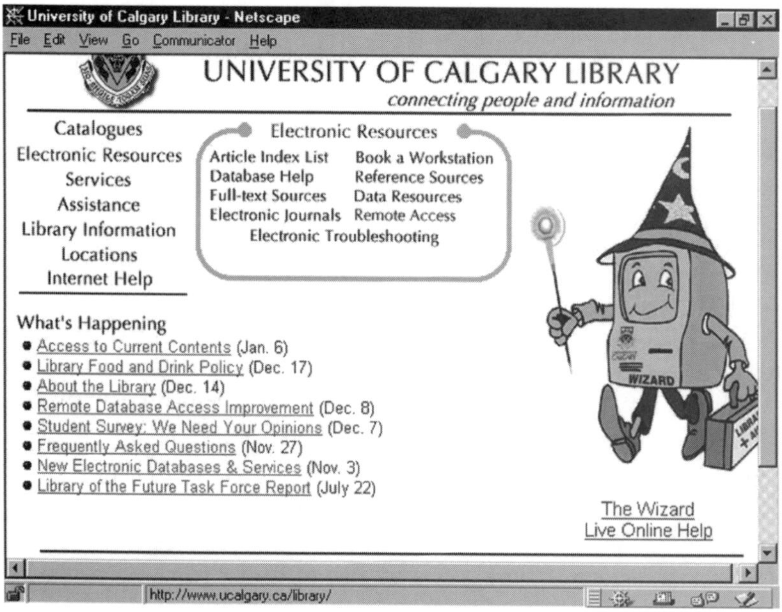

was loaded on each of the participating staff members' PCs so that service could be provided from their offices. An audio signal alerted the staff member to the receipt of a query. The success of this trial was directly attributable to the dedication and support of reference staff participating on the Wizard team as well as to the expertise and support provided by staff from Information Technology Services, a support unit within the library.

TRIAL RESULTS

While 31 questions were received during the fall trial, and 51 were received in the winter term, the system recorded far more connection attempts. These unsuccessful attempts were the result of researchers attempting to connect from nonsupported browsers. During the trial period, the software required Netscape 3.1 or Internet Explorer 4.x on Windows 95 or NT platforms. During the winter trial, a front-end screening process was implemented to warn people with incompatible browsers that they would not be able to access the service. Unfortunately, the

Figure 10. Trial information page

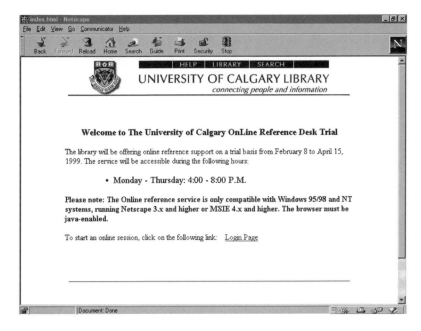

screening process was problematic, many times rejecting researchers who were clearly compatible. Fortunately, NEware has since been upgraded so that it will support pure html on all browsers 3.0 and up.

Questions received from researchers ranged from a request for help in connecting to the University of Calgary's Children's Literature Web Guide (*www.acs.ucalgary.ca/~dkbrown/*) to a request for assistance in locating material on the economic value of housework (see Appendix A for a list of questions received during the winter trial). The NEware software allows researchers and library staff "to converse" and enables library staff to send relevant documents and Web pages to the client (Figures 11 and 12). During the trial, logistics dictated that queries be answered exclusively with electronic resources available at the staff member's desktop. When print resources were required, researchers were asked to come into the library or told that they would be called or e-mailed the next day with the information.

Figure 11. Staff view (two questions being answered, one waiting to be taken)

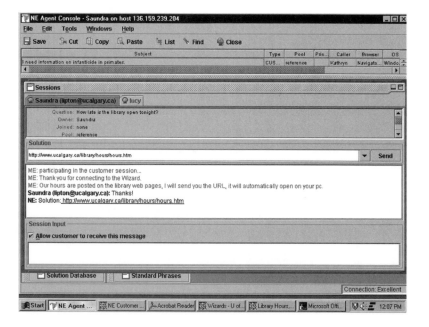

Figure 12. Users' view of a session

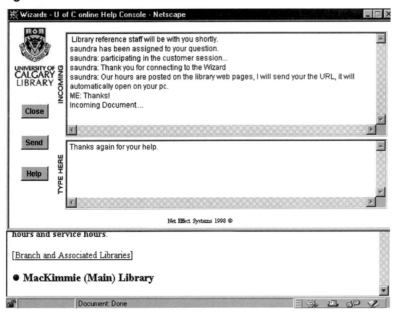

At the end of each session the client received a log of the session, including the URLs for the pages sent to them (Figure 13).

The software allows the library flexibility in setting the maximum number of questions that can be answered at one time; however, trying to deal with two clients at once was the maximum service capacity for each staff member (Figure 11). The system can also be set up so that numerous experts are available at any time and users can select where they want to direct the question. Alternatively, questions can be received centrally and be redirected to the appropriate expert. Staff members can share in taking questions and can consult with each other on questions or invite each other into the conversation with the client.

CLIENT FEEDBACK

Surveys were sent to all individuals who sent questions to the Wizard. The 23 surveys returned indicated strong support for the service. Comments received included:

- "Very quick service and very helpful."
- "Impressed by how smoothly it worked and the good results I got."
- "The wizard was a fantastic help. Made things easier for me."
- "Service was excellent, I was unable to find answers to my questions by browsing through the web pages. The Wizard provided those answers."

The respondents learned about the Wizard service primarily through the library Web pages, but also through posters and flyers and an article in the university newspaper. All accessed the Wizard from either their home or office PC.

A couple of individuals remarked on their preference to "talk" with the library staff; they felt that live conversation would have made it much easier to get an answer to their query. There was also some concern that this was not the most appropriate venue for dealing with difficult or complex information requests.

Figure 13. Session log

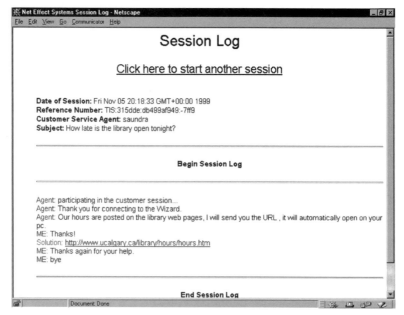

Almost all indicated that they chose the Wizard service because it seemed like a fast and convenient way to get library assistance.

ISSUES, CONCERNS, PROBLEMS

- For complex questions, it is often easiest to talk to the researcher over the phone or interact in person.
- The clients often "lost" the Wizard conversation box when we sent them a Web page.
- Conversation mode would be more effective if performed in real-time or ICQ chat; this way, the staff and the clients could see characters as they are being typed and the clients would know that someone is working on the answer. Conversation would be less stilted.
- There appeared to be a significant delay before the system indicated that a client had exited from the system. (Clients often did not say "good-bye.")
- Staff were unable to send Web pages to the client from within a catalog or database search session. It was possible only to copy and paste results and this format did not display well.

FUTURE DEVELOPMENTS

The survey responses revealed strong support for continuing this service. Most concerns with the software should be resolved with the new versions. Furthermore, the vendor has indicated that upcoming versions will allow co-browsing (the ability to "push" data to the client's desktop). Additionally, this software provides an option for providing desktop assistance, not only to researchers at their home or office PCs but also to the researchers utilizing the 200 or more PCs in the new Information Commons[2] (a central facility on campus providing access to information and technology support).

While users of the service and staff participating in the trial agreed that this is a valuable service, the level of demand was far too low to justify the continuation of real-time electronic reference as a separate service. As more and more resources become available electronically, allowing researchers to conduct more of their work at their desktop, it would be opportune to include desktop reference service as part of the new services being offered in the Information Commons; this would thus greatly enhance the availability of reference service. It is our plan in the coming year, resources permitting, to work towards integrating real-time electronic reference into the reference services provided in the Information Commons.

APPENDIX A

Questions Asked During the Winter Trial

Access Assistance

1. Can I get Proquest Direct from home?
2. Do you have the journal of American Ethnic History?
3. I am trying to find the ERIC database on the home page. Where is it?
4. I seem to remember that you had files on local actors that included reviews and the like. Is this true? and can I access it online?
5. I have been trying to access the user services online but every time I try, it says the session is already in use and I can't access through, is there something wrong with my system or yours?
6. I am currently on Sociofile. I want to put in a request to ILLO for some articles. How do I do it?
7. Logging onto remote access from Internet provider (not University of Calgary)—Do I use the id and password from U of C ID card?
8. I can't access Sociofile because the Webspirs link is not operating. Anything I can do about that?
9. How do I renew my books?
10. How do I access Medline?
11. I cannot seem to get into the site to renew my material. Am I doing something wrong?
12. What is my pin and userid?
13. Where can I pick up a copy of "ffwd" on or near campus?
14. I can't view details about journal articles from the advanced search page the MLA Resource Bibliography. Can you help me?
15. I am in MLA Bibliography through electronic resources link. The computer won't let me view search results
16. Is it possible to purchase UMI dissertations through Document Delivery Services at a reduced price (i.e., less than $36 US for Pb)?
17. Where are the Biology 305 marks posted on the net?

18. What job positions are available in the library?
19. Can you connect to the Social Sciences Index on the web?
20. Can't access Swetscan after login message appears.
21. As an Alumni with a valid library card can I put a reserve on checked-out books online for later pickup? Also, can I renew online books I have already checked out?
22. How do I take out videos and for how long can I have them out?
23. Can you please explain why when I try to renew books over the internet, I get a message "session already in use"?
24. How do I find if my hold is ready for pickup?
25. Looking for the Children's Literature Web
26. Hello, I seem to be having difficulty finding Sociofile
27. I'm trying to access Sociofile database; my ID and PIN are not being accepted.
28. Won't let me into database because it says my login is invalid but I don't think it is.
29. Are there special hours to access older journals that are on microfilm? What is the cost to get a paper copy?

Research Help

1. Chemotaxis in E. Coli?
2. Please advise where I would look for Human Resource Magazines
3. I'm having problems locating articles from 'normal' periodicals about the NHL
4. How to present a business offer for a business purchase to the seller
5. I am looking for articles on Samuel Beckett's Molloy
6. Training needs of soldiers and officers in the 21st century
7. Side effects of long term use of specific eye drops in treatment of glaucoma. Reference to ophthalmology journals will be fine. Thanks.
8. Doing a school project need information on certain jobs: Computer Engineering, Hardware Engineering, Software designer, Game designer
9. James Prescott Joule—information on life and works

10. Pictures of automobile hood ornaments
11. I am looking at the effects of MP 3's (a service provided on online of downloading songs from the net) on the economy. And how it worked then
12. I am looking for articles relating to how the book Satanic Verses was viewed by Canadian authorities
13. I am interested in researching the influences that make people either humanists or religious. Is this the kind of thing you can give help on?
14. I want to find the date of a ballad called Lord Randal
15. I am researching an organism called Tetraselmis. Can I obtain journal topics on the internet?
16. Is there anywhere on the library web pages I can find citation information?
17. Case summary and or analysis and commentary for Schachter v Canada a Supreme Court decision from 1992
18. Where would I look to see what rights a full-blooded Indian has?
19. I would like to verify academic qualifications. The person is xx who has a BSc in Computer Science from U of C. Year is uncertain but around 19xx.
20. Religion as power in ancient Greece and Rome, figures like Mark Antony, Caesar Cleopatra—need help on finding books on Greek and Roman Religion
21. Canada/US relations as they relate to Quebec's potential separation from Canada
22. Gender and parenting
23. Computer technology

NOTES

1. NetEffect Systems has since been acquired by Ask Jeeves (*www.ask.com*).
2. The Information Commons (*www.ucalgary.ca/IR/desktop.html*) is a central facility that integrates information resources with technology. This new facility was made possible by a $2.25 million grant received from Knowledge Networks, a government of Alberta initiative.

Conclusion

An Agenda
for Digital Reference

R. David Lankes

This chapter concludes the book by emphasizing the need for net-worked knowledge, in addition to digitization of secondary re-sources. It introduces a "primary knowledge revolution," where people are connected with experts and experience. Challenges are described such as scaling experts and routing questions to ap-propriate individuals. The changing role of librarians is explored, as evaluation of information and understanding the context of users' questions becomes more valuable than simply pointing us-ers to available resources.

A PRIMARY KNOWLEDGE REVOLUTION

Where do we go from here? The Internet has had a profound effect on the library. This is obvious if you use the library to surf the Net through public terminals. You have realized this if you search the library's online catalog through the Web. CD-ROM stations are being replaced with network access to full-text pe-riodicals, and endangered treasures, such as rare books and pho-tographs, are being rescued from oblivion with the aid of digi-tizing technology. Still more profound changes can be seen in digital libraries, massive collections of multimedia information on the Internet. However, these collection-based efforts are only the beginning. The next challenge for the library is to go beyond artifacts to true networked knowledge.

In the fifteenth century, Gutenberg started a secondary knowledge revolution. Through the printing press, Gutenberg allowed society to standardize how information was presented. The first book printed and the one-millionth book printed would be the same. Note that I said a "secondary" knowledge revolution. The book itself is not knowledge. True knowledge only resides with a person. True knowledge is a product of intelligence. You can interact with knowledge through dialog. You can pick at it, change it, and find its edges. Books, videos and the like only represent knowledge at a given point in time and only in one expression—thus, secondary knowledge. To date, the major impact of the Internet in libraries has been a continuation of the secondary knowledge revolution. We take expressions of knowledge and put them into digital format.

We stand on the edge of a primary knowledge revolution. In this revolution, rather than networking books, we network authors. In this revolution we talk about how to represent people, experts and expertise, not documents. In this revolution we go past the painting to the artist, past the headlines to the journalist, past the journal to the scientist. At the end of this revolution we will not have huge structures, or massive shelving of paper and leather. At the end of this revolution we will have developed a sort of global brain. A new networked extended memory that will allow us to tap into direct experience and understanding.

There is a catch. Networking human beings makes the problems of networking digital objects seem trivial by comparison. How do you scale an expert? If a library needs a book that is checked out, it can simply buy another copy. If a Website gets a lot of traffic, one can add a faster computer. On the other hand, if an expert receives a large number of questions, one can't simply add a clone (at least not yet). How do you route questions to the most appropriate expert? If you are given two experts of equal stature, how do you pick one? Possibly a more cogent question to this forum is: what is the role of the library and librarians in this environment?

THE LIBRARIAN: CHANGING ROLES AND SKILLS

Just as Gutenberg's revolution did not displace what had come before (oral histories, live performances, debates), so too the primary knowledge revolution will work in concert with the secondary knowledge revolution. We will still read books; we will still need Web pages and videos. These resources are more scalable and convenient. So one role (I would argue the minor role) of the revolutionized librarian will be to maintain and organize objects (both physical and digital).

Now, however, we can infuse real understanding and dialog into our libraries. Now our libraries' stacks are lined not only with books and paper, but understanding, experts, and people. As the library's collection changes so too must the librarian's role. In the secondary knowledge world before networking and digitization, the library had to collect a large amount and variety of information objects (traditionally books). The role of the reference librarian was to guide users through the collection. That is, the collection of materials housed at a given library.

Now with digital objects and networked collections, where one could define a library's collection to contain the entire content of the Internet (for good and bad), the role changes. The role of the reference librarian is now not to simply point out relevant information to a patron, but to point out the "best" resources. This is a key difference. When there are potentially millions of relevant articles, Websites, and videos on a topic, no one has time to sift through it. Instead people will turn to trusted intermediaries to pick resources that are useful. These trusted intermediaries will be librarians.

Librarians are trained information brokers. They are trained in finding information and evaluating information. While we currently look to librarians to help us find information, it is evaluating information that will ultimately prove to be the more valuable skill. What will bring a patron (physically or virtually) to a given library will be the context that a library or librarian provides. Librarians in the future will become context experts. They will build on their current reference skills. These skills are not simply understanding given sources (often content experts know the sources better), but the ability to read the situation a user is in and find the right information for that situation. The skill a reference librarian must develop is that of environmental scanning, not topical identification (in other words, understanding *why* someone asks a question, not simply *what* they are asking about).

A CALL TO REVOLUTION

I invite you into the revolution. I invite you to be a reference revolutionary. Stop looking at a library as a collection of objects and start seeing it as a house of contexts. Stop looking at librarians as information custodians, and demand they be guides. I invite you to invent the future!

Appendix

Digital Reference Resources

Compiled by Joann M. Wasik

The following list contains bibliographic references to resources on the topic of digital reference in a variety of contexts. This resource list will be updated regularly online at: *www.vrd.org/ pubinfo/proceedings99_bib.html*

GENERAL LIBRARY AND EDUCATION

Anderson, C. "Using Technology: The Electronic Reference Desk." *Wilson Library Bulletin* 64 (1989): 86–87+.

"Ask a Librarian: Thirteen Great Websites for Grown-ups." *Children's Software Revue* 14 (May/June 1998).

Auster, E. "User Satisfaction with the Online Negotiation Interview: Contemporary Concern in Traditional Perspective." *RQ* 23, no. 1 (1983): 47–59.

Bennett, B. A. "KidsConnect: Teacher-Librarians Helping Kids Solve Their Information Problems on the Internet." *The Teaching Librarian* 4, no. 3 (1997): 14–17.

Bennett, B. A. "Gendered Questions: Asking for Directions on the Information Highway." *Knowledge Quest* 2, no. 2 (1998): 24–25.

Bennett, B. A. "Handling the Quirky Questions: A Model for Reference Service." *Knowledge Quest* 26, no. 2 (1998): 59–60.

Bennett, B. A. Developing an Internet-Based Reference Service. Pp. 159–69 in *The Cybrarian's Manual 2*, edited by Pat Ensor. Chicago: American Library Association, 2000.

Bry, L. Setting up an Ask-an-Expert Service. [Online.] 1997. Available: *www.madsci.org/ask_expert/index.html* [24 March 2000].

Coffman, S. "Reference as Others Do It." *American Libraries* 30, no. 5 (1999): 54–56.

Coffman, S. and M. L. Saxton, "Staffing the Reference Desk in the Largely-Digital Library." *Reference Librarian* 66 (1999): 141–61.

Cowan, H. "'Ask-the-Expert' Internet Sites." *Electronic Learning* 16, no. 3 (1996): 22.

Ekhaml, L. "Ask an Expert with Style." *School Library Media Activities Monthly* 15, no. 6 (1999): 27–30.

Foster, S. Guide to Writing Responses. [Online.] 1998. Available: *http://forum.swarthmore.edu/dr.math/guide/* [24 March 2000].

Guernsey, L. "Suddenly, Everybody's an Expert on Everything." *The New York Times*, 3 February 1999, sec. G1. [Online.] Available: *www.nytimes.com/library/tech/00/02/circuits/articles/03info.html* [24 March 2000].

Hays, C. L. "Help for the Homework Challenged." *The New York Times*, 6 April 1997, sec. 4A, 15–16, 20.

Hulshof, R. "Providing Services to Virtual Patrons." *Information Outlook* 3, no. 1 (1999): 20–23.

Irwin, K. R. "Professional Reference Service at the Internet: Public Library with 'Freebie' Librarians." *Searcher* 6, no. 9 (1998): 21–23.

Kasowitz, A. S. Facets of Quality for K–12 Digital Reference Services. [Online.] 1997. Available: *www.vrd.org/training/facets.html* [20 February 2000].

Kasowitz, A. S. AskA Service Question Submission Forms. [Online.] 1998. Available: *www.vrd.org/AskA/askaforms.html* [3 March 2000].

Kasowitz, A. S. Guidelines for Information Specialists of K–12 Digital Reference Services. [Online.] 1998. Available: *www.vrd.org/training/guide.htm* [10 March 2000].

Kasowitz, A. S. Promoting Information Problem Solving in Digital Reference Responses. [Online.] 1998. Available: *www.vrd.org/training/ips.html* [10 March 2000].

Koyama, J. T. *"http://digiref.scenarios.issues."* *Reference & User Services Quarterly* 38, no. 1 (1998): 51–53.

LaBounty, V. "Reference Desk on the Internet." *Book Report* 16, no. 2 (1997): 19.

Lankes, R. D. "AskERIC: The Virtual Librarian." *Information Searcher* 6, no. 1 (1993): 20–22.

Lankes, R. D. "AskERIC and the Virtual Library: Lessons for Emerging Digital Libraries." *Internet Research* 5, no. 1 (1995): 56–63.

Lankes, R. D. "AskA's: Lessons Learned from K-12 Digital Reference Services." *Reference & User Services Quarterly* 38, no. 1 (1998): 63–71.

Lankes, R. D. *Building and Maintaining Internet Information Services: K–12 Digital Reference Services*. Syracuse, N.Y.: ERIC Clearinghouse on Information & Technology, 1998.

Lankes, R. D. The Virtual Reference Desk: Building Human Expertise into Information Systems. Pp. 81-90 in *Proceedings of the ASIS Annual Meeting*, Vol. 35. Medford, N.J.: Information Today, 81–90. (1998).

Lankes, R. D. Virtual Reference Desk Interviews. [Online.] 1998. Available: *www.vrd.org/AskA/interviews.html* [10 March 2000].

Lankes, R. D. and A. S. Kasowitz. *The AskA Starter Kit: How to Build and Maintain Digital Reference Services*. Syracuse, N.Y.: ERIC Clearinghouse on Information & Technology, 1998.

"Librarians Meet to Turn Online Services into 'Virtual' Certainty." *Wilson Library Bulletin* 69 (1995): 17.

MAD Scientist Network. The MadSci Moderators' Manual. [Online.] 1997. Available: *www.madsci.org/ask_expert/moderators.html* [24 March 2000].

MAD Scientist Network. The Mad Scientist Network: User's Manual. [Online.] 1997. Available: *www.madsci.org/ask_expert/exp_manual.html* [24 March 2000].

Mahony, A. P. "The Net and Reference Services: Capture the Question." *Wilson Library Bulletin* 69, no. 2 (1993): 12.

McKee, M. B. "A Day in the Life of a Virtual Librarian." *School Library Journal* 41, no. 4 (1995): 30–33.

Myers, J. E. "Reference Services in the Virtual Library: What's in Store for the Next Decade." *American Libraries* 25 (1994): 634–38.

Ormes, S. "Feature: Ask a Librarian." *Library Technology* 3, no. 2 (1998). [Online.] Available: *www.sbu.ac.uk/litc/lt/1998/news619.html* [11 March 2000].

Papandrea, V. A. "Managing Reference Services in the Electronic Age: A Competing Values Approach to Effectiveness." *Reference Librarian* 60 (1998): 111–26.

Pearlman, R. "NSS On-line: 'Ask an Astronaut' Scores Major Success." *Ad Astra* 8 (1996): 8–9.

Philip, B. *mayihelpyou@theelectronicreferencedesk?* An Examination of the Past, Present and Future of Electronic Mail Reference Service. [Online.] 1997. Available: *http://hollyhock.slis.ualberta.ca/598/brenda/emailref.htm* [24 March 2000].

Quint, B. "Round the Clock, Round the World." *Information Today* 15, no. 6 (1998): 8.

Sell, D. *Utilizing a Rapid Prototyping Approach in the Building of a Hypermedia-Based Reference Station.* Syracuse, N.Y.: ERIC Clearinghouse on Information & Technology, 1994.

Schaefer, M. T. "Landmark Digital Age Reference Service Institute Inaugurated by Library of Congress: Part 1: Key Digiref Concerns." *Information Retrieval & Library Automation* 34, no. 3 (1998): 1–3.

Schaefer, M. T. "Landmark LC Institute, Part 2: Real Virtual Information Service Issues." *Information Retrieval & Library Automation* 34, no. 4 (1998): 1–5.

Sloan, B. "Service Perspectives for the Digital Library: Remote Reference Services." *Library Trends* 47, no. 1 (1998): 117–143. Available: *www.lis.uiuc.edu/~sloan/e-ref.html* [24 February 2000].

Stahl, J. R. "'Have a Question? Click Here': Electronic Reference at the National Museum of American Art." *Art Documentation* 17, no. 1 (1998): 10–12.

Steinberg, J. "'Do the Math?' Sure, with Help Online." *The New York Times,* 15 October 1998, sec. G10.

Summers, R. "Meeting Education Information Needs through Digital Reference." *Art Documentation* 17, no. 1 (1998): 3–4, 68.

Tennant, R. "Of Human and Humane Assistance." *Library Journal* 124, no. 11 (1999): 30–34.

Tobiason, K. "Taking by Giving: KidsConnect and Your Media Center." *Technology Connection* 4, no. 6 (1997): 10–11.

Tomer, L. "MIME and Electronic Reference Services." *The Reference Librarian* 41/42 (1994): 347–73.

Viles, A. The Virtual Reference Interview: Equivalencies. Discussion Proposal Distributed at the International Federation of Library Associations and Institutions (IFLA) Discussion Group on Reference Work, Bangkok. [Online.] 1999. Available: *www.ifla.org/VII/dg/dgrw/dp99-06.htm* [22 March 2000].

Virtual Reference Desk. Using AskA Services with Students. [Online.] 1999. Available: *www.vrd.org/k12/k12FAQ.html* [10 February 2000].

Wasik, J. M. AskA Services and Funding: An Overview. [Online.] 1998. Available: *www.vrd.org/AskA/aska_funding.html* [20 February 2000].

Wasik, J. M. A Report of Library-Related AskA Services. [Online.] 1998. Available: *www.vrd.org/AskA/library.html* [20 February 2000].

Wasik, J. M. "Building and Maintaining Digital Reference Services." *ERIC Digest*, 1999. [Online.] Available: *http://ericir.syr.edu/ithome/digests/digiref.html* [3 March 2000].

Wasik, J. M. and Lankes, R. D. The Virtual Reference Desk: Supporting Education through a Network of Human Expertise. Pp. 198–202 in *Internet Librarian '99 Conference Proceedings*. Medford, N.J.: Information Today, Inc., 1999.

Wasman, W. "Ask Dr. Dino; or, My Life as an Electronic Reptile." *American Libraries* 24 (1993): 122–23.

Watstein, S. B. "Reference Service in a Digital Age." *Library Hi-Tech News* 155 (1998): 9.

ACADEMIC LIBRARIES

Abels, E. G. and P. Liebscher. Intermediary-Client Communication: Provision of Remote Reference Services. Pp 1-7 in *IOLS '94: Proceedings of the Ninth Annual Conference on Integrated Online Library Systems*. Medford, N.J.: Learned Information, Inc., 1994.

Barnes, S. J. "The Electronic Library and Public Services." *Library Hi Tech* 12, no. 3 (1994): 44–62.

Billings, H., I. E. Carver, and D. Racine. "Remote Reference Assistance for Electronic Information Resources over Networked Workstations." *Library Hi Tech* 12, no. 1 (1994): 77–86.

Borgendale, M. and F. O. Weise. "EARS: Electronic Access to Reference Service." *Bulletin of the Medical Library Association* 74, no. 4 (1986): 300–4.

Bristow, A. "Academic Reference Service over Electronic Mail." *College & Research Libraries News* 53 (1992): 631–32.

Bristow, A. and M. Buechley. "Academic Reference Service over E-mail: An Update." *College & Research Libraries News* 7 (1995): 459–62.

Bushallow-Wilbur, L., G. S. DeVinney, and F. Whitcomb. "Electronic Mail Reference Service: A Study." *RQ*, 35, no. 3 (1996): 359–71.

Cargill, J. S. "The Electronic Reference Desk: Reference Service in an Electronic World." *Library Administration & Management* 6, no. 2 (1992): 82–85.

Fishman, D. L. "Managing the Virtual Reference Desk: How to Plan an Effective Reference E-mail System." *Medical Reference Services Quarterly* 17, no. 1 (1998): 1–10.

Frank, I. B. "E-mail Reference Service at the University of South Florida: A Well-Kept Secret." *Art Documentation* 17, no. 1 (1998): 8–9, 44.

Hahn, K. An Investigation of an E-mail-Based Help Service. [Online.] 1997. Available: *www.clis.umd.edu/research/reports/tr97/03/9703.html* [3 March 2000].

Hatfield, V. S. The Electronic Library's Impact on Reference Service. In *Community College Reference Services*, edited by Bill Katz. Lanham, Md.: Scarecrow Press, 1992.

Jackson, J. and B. Parton. "Virtual Reference Desk for Regional Education Center Libraries. *Illinois Libraries* 81, no. 1 (1999): 39–41.

Jensen, A. M. and J. Sih. "Using E-mail and the Internet to Teach Users at Their Desktops." *Online* 19 (1995): 82–86.

Kim, H., T. Ahn, and B. Kwok. VINIS: The WWW Virtual Reference Librarian System. Pp 33-43 in *Digital Libraries and Information Services for the 21st Century Conference Proceedings*. Seoul, Korea: Koliss, 1996.

Kisby, C., M. Kilman, and C. Hinshaw. "Extended Reference Service in the Electronic Environment." *Information Technology and Libraries* 18, no. 2 (1999): 92–95.

Mendelsohn, J. "Perspectives on Quality of Reference Service in an Academic Library: A Qualitative Study." *RQ* 36, no. 4 (1997): 544–57.

Pal, G., J. Brett, and T. Flemming. "Providing Electronic Library Reference Service: Experiences from the Indonesia-Canada Tele-Education Project." *The Journal of Academic Librarianship* 15 (1989): 274–78.

Sloan, B. "Electronic Reference Services." *Reference & User Services Quarterly* 38, no.1 (1998): 77–81.

Sloan, B. Library Support for Distance Learning. [Online.] n.d. Available: *http://alexia.lis.uiuc.edu/~b-sloan/libdist.htm*. (13 March 2000).

Sloan, B. E-mail Reference Sites. [Online.] 1999. Available: *www.lis.uiuc.edu/~b-sloan/e-mail.html*. (13 March 2000).

Still, J., and F. Campbell. "Librarian in a Box: The Use of Electronic Mail for Reference. *Reference Services Review* 21, no. 1 (1993): 15–18.

Tillman, H. Electronic Reference Service on Jumbonet. Pp 231–36 in *IOLS '90, Integrated Online Library Systems*. Medford, N.J.: Learned Information, 1990.

PUBLIC LIBRARIES

Carter, D. S. IPL Reference from the Inside Out: An Overview of IPL Reference. [Online.] 1998. Available: *www.ipl.org:2000/backroom/training/talks/ref.html* [21 March 2000].

Hegenbart, B. "The Economics of the Internet Public Library." *Library Hi Tech* 16, no. 2 (1998).

Janes, J. "The Internet Public Library: An Intellectual History." *Library Hi Tech* 16, no. 2 (1998).

Janes, J., D. Carter, A. Lagace, M. McLennen, S. Ryan, S. Simcox. *The Internet Public Library Handbook*. New York: Neal-Schuman Publishers, 1999.

Lagace, N. "The Internet Public Library's 'Ask A Question Worldwide Reference Service.'" *Art Documentation* 17, no. 1 (1998): 5–7.

Lagace, N. and M. McClennen. "Questions and Quirks." *Computers in Libraries*, 18, no. 2 (1998): 24–27. [Online.] Available: *www.infotoday.com/cilmag/feb98/story1.htm* [22 March 2000].

Lee, K. "E-mail Reference Service...HUH?" *Indiana Libraries* 15, no. 2 (1996): 57–61.

McClure, C. R. "A Planning Primer for Online Reference Service in a Public Library." *Online* 4, no. 2 (1980): 57–65.

McDermott, I. E. "Virtual Reference for a Real Public." *Searcher* 6, no. 4 (1998): 25–31.

McWilliams, A. "Electronic Reference Sources and Reference Service." *Colorado Libraries* 23 (1997): 43–44.

Neff, P. "Virtual Librarianship: Expanding Adult Services with the World Wide Web." *RQ* 35 (1995): 169–72.

Ormes, S. Public Libraries Corner: Ask a Librarian. *Ariadne* 13 (1998). [Online.] Available: *www.ariadne.ac.uk/issue13/public-libraries/* [24 March 2000].

Pack, T. "A Guided Tour of the Internet Public Library: Cyberspace's Unofficial Library Offers Outstanding Collections of Internet Resources." *Database* 19, no. 5 (1996): 52–56.

Reger, N. K. "Redefining Reference Services." *Reference & User Services Quarterly* 38, no. 1 (1998): 73.

Reid, J.A. "Electronic Reference Service at Jefferson County [Colorado] Public Libraries." *Library Software Review* 10 (1991): 404–5.

Ryan, S. "Reference Service for the Internet Community: A Case Study of the Internet Public Library Reference Division." *Library & Information Science Research* 18, no. 3 (1996): 241–59.

"Serving the Internet Public: The Internet Public Library." *Electronic Library* 14, no. 2 (1996): 122–26.

Whitwell, S. C. "Internet Public Library: Same Metaphors, New Service." *American Libraries* 28, no. 2 (1997): 56–59.

SPECIAL LIBRARIES

Howard, E. H. and T. A. Jankowski. "Reference Services via Electronic Mail." *Bulletin of the Medical Library Association* 74 (1986): 41–44.

Kaczor, S. A. "Reference Service in an Electronic Age: A View from Two Worlds Based on an SLA Program." *Technicalities* 15 (March 1995): 1+.

Keselica, M. "The 'People' Part of Groupware." *Online* 18 (1994): 104–5.

Rich, J. L. *Effective Information Delivery: Information for Management.* Washington, DC: Special Library Association, 1994.

GOVERNMENT INFORMATION SERVICES/CENTERS

Hattery, M. "Reference Service in a Digital Age: Three Projects." *Information Retrieval & Library Automation* 34, no. 9 (1999): 1–2.

Hull, T. and M. O. Adams. "Electronic Communications for Reference Services: A Case Study." *Government Information Quarterly* 12, no. 3 (1995): 297–308.

Kresh, D. and L. Arret. "Do Birds Fly?: Some Thoughts after the Library of Congress Institute on 'Reference Service in a Digital Age.'" *Reference & User Services Quarterly* 38, no. 1 (1998): 17–21.

GENERAL DIGITAL REFERENCE RESEARCH

Abels, E. G. "The E-mail Reference Interview." *RQ* 35, no. 3 (1996): 345–58.

Bunge, C. A. "Factors Related to Reference Question Answering Success: The Development of a Data-Gathering Form." *RQ* (Summer 1985): 482–86.

Crews, K. D. "The Accuracy of Reference Service: Variables for Research and Implementation." *LISR* 10 (1988): 331–55.

Davenport, E. and R. Procter. The Situated Intermediary: Remote Advice Giving in a Distributed Reference Environment. In *Proceedings of the Eighteenth National Online Meeting.* Medford, N.J.: Information Today (1997).

Ferguson, C. D. and C. A. Bunge. "The Shape of Services to Come: Values-Based Reference Service for the Largely Digital Library." *College & Research Libraries* 58 (1997): 252–65.

Lipow, A. G. "Thinking out Loud: Who Will Give Reference Service in the Digital Environment?" *Reference & User Services Quarterly* 37, no. 2 (1997): 125–29.

Lipow, A. G. Serving the Remote User: Reference Service in the Digital Environment. Pp. 106–26 in *Proceedings of the Australasian Information Online & On Disc Conference,* 1999. [Online.] Available: *www.csu.au/special/online99/proceedings99/200.htm* [15 February 2000].

Saxton, M. L. "Reference Service Evaluation and Meta-Analysis: Findings and Methodological Issues. *Library Quarterly* 67, no. 3 (1997): 267–89.

BUSINESS

Jessup, L. M. n.d. Enterprise-wide Brainstorming on the Web: The Case of Experts Exchange. [Online.] Available: *http://php.indiana.edu/~ljessup/gwcent4.html* [3 March 2000]

Kay, A. S. "Call Centers Meet the Web." *LAN Times* 14, no. 25 (8 December 1997): 41–42.

Maney, K. "Site to Auction Information." *USA Today*, 9 September 1999. [Online.] Available: *http://www.usatoday.com/life/cyber/tech/ctg076.htm* [24 March 2000].

Nelson, M. "Trio Looks to Customer Service." *InfoWorld* 20, no. 23 (8 June 1998): 63.

O'Connell, P. L. "We Got Your E-mail; Just Don't Expect a Reply. *The New York Times*, 6 July 1998, sec. D3.

Sterne, J. "Minding the Mail." *CIO Web Business* 30 (1 May 1998): 32.

Wasik, J. M. Information for Sale: Commercial Digital Reference and AskA Services. [Online.] 1999. Available: *http://www.vrd.org/AskA/commAskA.html* (8 March 2000).

REAL TIME PROJECTS AND TECHNOLOGIES

D'Angelo, B. J. and B. M. Maid. Service from a Distance: The Use of Information Technologies in Support of Off-campus Students. *Proceedings from CAUSE 98*, 1998. [Online.] Available: *www.educause.edu/ir/library/html/cnc9847/cnc9847.html* (22 March 2000).

Henderson, T. A. "MOOving Towards a Virtual Reference Service." *The Reference Librarian* 41–42 (1994): 173–84.

Lessick, S., K. Kjaer, and S. Clancy. Interactive Reference Service (IRS) at UC Irvine: Expanding Reference Service beyond the Reference Desk. [Online.] 1997. Available: *www.ala.org/acrl/paperhtm/a10.html* [24 March 2000]

"Michigan Offers Videoconference Access to Reference Librarian." *Chronicle of Higher Education*, 26 July 1996, sec. A21.

Pagell, R. A. "The Virtual Reference Librarian: Using Desktop Videoconferencing for Distance Reference." *Electronic Library* 14, no. 1 (1996): 21-26.

Tinnin, N., J. Buckstead, and K. Richardson. Remote Reference by Microcomputer: Setup and Installation. Pp. 299–312 in *Proceedings of the Off-Campus Library Services Conference 1998*, Vol. 1.

Westwood, K. "Lights! Camera! Action!" *American Libraries* 28, no. 1 (1997): 43–45.

About the Contributors

JOSEPH JANES

Joseph Janes, Ph.D., is assistant professor at the School of Library and Information Science at the University of Washington and is founding director of the Internet Public Library. A frequent speaker in the United States and abroad, he is the co-author of seven books on librarianship, technology, and their relationship, including the new *Internet Public Library Handbook*. He holds an M.L.S. and Ph.D. from Syracuse University, and has taught at the University of Michigan, the University of North Carolina at Chapel Hill, the State University of New York at Albany, Syracuse University, and the University of Washington.

SUSAN LESSICK

Susan Lessick is Acting Assistant University Librarian for Research and Instructional Services at the University of California, Irvine where she has held various positions, including Head of Research and Instructional Services at the Science Library and Head of the Medical Center Library. She has expertise in applying new technologies and models to improve reference and instructional services. She has made numerous regional and national presentations on reference service trends, issues, and innovations.

LORNA PETERSON

Lorna Peterson is associate professor at the School of Library and Information Studies at the State University of New York at Buffalo. She teaches in the areas of reference, social science reference, bibliographic instruction, and international publishing. She received a B.A. from Dickinson College, an M.L.S. from Case Western Reserve University, and a Ph.D. in Education from Iowa State University. Peterson has published in the areas of reference services, bibliographic instruction, and multicultural issues in librarianship.

MYOUNG C. WILSON

Myoung Chung Wilson is information services librarian/library liaison to the School of Communication, Information and Library Studies (SCILS) at Rutgers, the State University of New Jersey. She has held several leadership positions as head of public services and head of collection development and management at Rutgers' Alexander Library. She currently serves as chair of the Rutgers New Brunswick Libraries Information Services Group. Her research addresses issues of information access. She is the current chair of the Social Science Libraries Section of the International Federation of Library Associations and Institutions. She received her B.A. from Ewha Women's University in Seoul, Korea, an M.A. from Pennyslvania State University and her M.L.S. from the University of Michigan.

DIANE KRESH

Diane Kresh is Director for Public Service Collections and Director for Preservation at the Library of Congress (LC). Her experience at LC has covered a wide spectrum of responsibilities, including copyright, collections maintenance, document delivery, reference, user training, photoduplication services, and conservation. Diane serves on the LC Internet Policy Committee, directs nearly all the Library's general and special collections, and is leading the effort to provide enhanced Internet services for public researchers.

LINDA ARRET

Linda Arret is a network specialist in the Library of Congress Network Development and MARC Standards Office, where she focuses on issues related to reference and public services. Linda's experience as a frontline reference librarian has been instrumental in projects she has helped lead and plan, including online catalog development, public access to the Internet, public and staff training programs, reference presence on the Web, and collaborative efforts for providing digital reference services.

BLYTHE ALLISON BENNETT

Blythe Allison Bennett is the Virtual Reference Desk Learning Center Coordinator and works at the Information Institute of Syracuse at Syracuse University. Before joining the VRD project, she coordinated the KidsConnect project, an Internet based Q&A project for K–12 students. Blythe was a high school Spanish teacher, sixth grade teacher, and elementary school librarian. She earned her M.L.S. from Syracuse University and her bachelor's degrees from Marietta College.

PAULINE LYNCH

Pauline coordinates the AskERIC question–answering service and its team of information specialists. AskERIC Q&A is an electronic service providing research assistance to anyone interested in the process or practice of education. Pauline earned her B.S. in psychology and elementary teacher certification from LeMoyne College and received her M.L.S. at Syracuse University. Pauline has worked at various libraries and school districts in the Syracuse, New York area.

BRETT BUTLER

Brett Butler is the president of Infour and the publisher of AnswerBase, a new reference information system. He has been licensing digital data since 1984, when Information Access, of which he was founding president, began to build online databases for distribution through DIALOG. He has been a database publisher, librarian, and bookseller and has spoken and written widely in the education community and information industry.

LYNN BRY

Lynn Bry, M.D., Ph.D., is currently a resident physician in the Department of Pathology at Brigham & Women's Hospital at Harvard Medical School in Boston, Massachusetts. While a student in the Medical Scientist Training Program at Washington University School of Medicine in St. Louis, she founded and continues to direct the MAD Scientist Network, a Web-based Ask-A-Scientist service.

BRUCE HENSON

Bruce Henson is reference librarian at Georgia Tech Library. He received a B.A. from Mary Baldwin College in Staunton, Virginia and an M.L.S. from the University of North Carolina at Chapel Hill. Henson worked as a media technician at Central Virginia Community College for over a decade before attending graduate school.

JUDY HORN

Judy Horn is head of the Government Information Department at the University of California, Irvine and co-chair of the Research and Instruction Division of the Electronic Reference Service Team.

KATHRYN KJAER

Kathryn Kjaer is acting head of the Research and Instruction Department at the Science Library at University of California, Irvine. She is co-chair of the Research and Instruction Division of the Electronic Reference Service Team.

MARILYN DOMAS WHITE

Marilyn Domas White is an associate professor at the College of Library and Information Services (CLIS) at the University of Maryland in the area of information access. One area of research interest is information-seeking behavior, particularly how people express information needs through questioning behavior. She has recently published two studies of questioning behavior in different settings: in reference interviews preceding online searches and on consumer health-related electronic lists. She is currently analyzing questions from several different digital reference services. She taught a course on electronic question-answer services and edited "Analyzing Electronic Question/Answer Services: Framework and Evaluations of Selected Services," CLIS Technical Report no. 99–01 (July 1999).

LAURA SOWERS

Laura Sowers is a reference librarian for GCI Information Services at the Census Bureau Library. This research was done while she was a graduate student in the College of Library and Information Services, University of Maryland. In her program she was a University of Maryland Graduate Fellow. She worked as a volunteer at the National Museum of American Art's Reference Desk and, as a graduate assistant, helped to create the electronic reference service at McKeldin Library, University of Maryland. She is an honors graduate in art history from William and Mary College and worked in the art department's slide library as an undergraduate student.

SUSAN MCGLAMERY

Susan McGlamery is the reference coordinator for the Metropolitan Cooperative Library System, and has an extensive history managing reference services in legal, corporate, and public library environments.

STEVE COFFMAN

Steve Coffman is product development manager of Library Sytems and Services, Inc. He is the former director of FYI, the fee-based business information service of the County of Los Angeles Public Library. His work includes development of innovative approaches to providing reference and research services in public libraries. Steve is the author of several library trade journal articles including "Building Earth's Largest Library," "Reference As Others Do It," and "What if You Ran Your Library Like a Bookstore." He is the editor of ALA's *Internet Plus Directory of Express Library Services* and is impresario and program developer for the Southern California Online Users Group. Steve earned his M.L.S. from UCLA in 1985, and a B.A. in foreign languages from San Francisco State University.

MONIKA ANTONELLI

Monika Antonelli is general reference librarian at the University of North Texas Libraries in Denton, Texas. During the past three years, she has presented innovative programs at the annual conferences of American Library Association, Texas Library Association, and Oregon Library Association. She currently serves as a book and Website reviewer for *Choice*. In her free time, she volunteers as a Web editor for the Open Directory Project (*http://dmoz.org/*).

MARTHA TARLTON

Martha Tarlton is head of Humanities and Social Sciences at the University of North Texas Libraries. She is very active in the Texas Library Association, serving as Chair of Reference Round Table and holding other offices and committee appointments. She has had several bibliographic essays published in *Serials Review* and serves as a contributor to ARBA. Martha is a member of ALA, ACRL, and RUSA.

SAUNDRA LIPTON

Saundra Lipton is the manager of reference services and library research services at the University of Calgary Library in Calgary, Alberta. She holds additional responsibilities as the liaison librarian for Religious Studies and Philosophy and has over 20 years of experience as a reference librarian. Saundra helps maintain the Religious Studies Web Guide (*www.ucalgary.ca/~lipton*).

About the Editors

R. DAVID LANKES

R. David Lankes, Ph.D., is Director of the Information Institute of Syracuse (IIS) and an Assistant Professor at Syracuse University's School of Information Studies. Lankes received his B.F.A. (Multimedia Design), M.S. in Telecommunications and Ph.D. from Syracuse University.

Lankes is co-founder of the award-winning AskERIC project, an Internet service for educators, and founder of the Virtual Reference Desk, a project building a national network of expertise for education. Lankes is also one of the architects of GEM, a standards-based system for describing and finding educational materials on the Internet. Lankes' research is in education information and digital reference services. He has authored, co-authored, or edited four books and has written numerous book chapters and journal articles on the Internet and digital reference. He speaks and consults nationally on Internet issues in education and business.

JOHN W. COLLINS III

John Collins, Ed.D., is librarian for the Harvard Graduate School of Education (HGSE) and a member of the Faculty of Education. He directs the Monroe C. Gutman Library, which maintains collections of 160,000 volumes and over 2,000 journal titles and provides a full range of research support services to the HGSE community. He is a specialist in information technology and serves on several national boards and task forces. He recently completed work designing a new National Library of Education and is currently consulting with the U.S. Department of Education in developing and implementing the National Education Network. He is a trustee of a local public library and a regular reviewer for several library journals. He is also deeply involved with campuswide efforts toward implementing the next generation of the Harvard On-Line Library Information System. He received his Ed.D. from Boston University.

ABBY S. KASOWITZ

Abby Kasowitz is Coordinator of the Virtual Reference Desk (VRD) Project, a special project of the ERIC Clearinghouse on Information and Technology, part of the Information Institute of Syracuse (IIS). Abby is co-author of the *AskA Starter Kit: How to Build and Maintain Digital Reference Services*. In her role as VRD Coordinator, Abby plans an annual national conference on Internet-based reference service for library and information professionals; researches the digital reference field; and assists organizations in building digital reference services. Abby presents on the Virtual Reference Desk Project and digital reference at meetings and conferences nationally.

Abby received her M.L.S. and M.S. in Instructional Design, Development and Evaluation from Syracuse University and her B.A. in English and American Literature from Brandeis University. She joined IIS in 1997 as an assistant with KidsConnect, an Internet-based question/answer and referral service for K–12 students.

Index